The Wishing Handbook

More Than 500 Ways to Make Your Wishes Come True

by Gloria T. Delamar

RUNNING PRESS
PHILADELPHIA · LONDON

Printed in China

9   8   7   6   5   4   3   2   1
Digit on the right indicates the number of this printing

Library of Congress Cataloging-in-Publication Number 98-68478

ISBN 0-7624-0540-6

Cover illustration by Hadyn Cornner
Cover design by Frances J. Soo Ping Chow
Edited by Caroline E. Tiger
Typography: Fairfield, and School Script

The following used by permission:
"The Wish in Transition" © Keltcie M. Delamar
"A Wish Can Be" © William T. Delamar
"Wishing" © Joan Grady-Fitchett
"The Magic of Wishing" © Ethel S. Oliver
"Limerick: Princess 'Capricious'" © Judy Tucker

This book may be ordered by mail from the publisher.
Please include $2.50 for postage and handling.
But try your bookstore first!

Running Press Book Publishers
125 South Twenty-second Street
Philadelphia, Pennsylvania 19103-4399

Visit us on the web!
www.runningpress.com

Dedication

For WTD, in my heart always;
the miracle five we watched grow,
the significant others who share their lives and thus ours,
and the three grandurchins.
All of you are everything for which I could ever wish.

Acknowledgments

Thank you to so many friends, acquaintances, and even strangers who generously shared wishing customs. In particular, I wish to thank those who, inspired by the concept that wishing enriches our lives, gave permission for the inclusion of original work.

—GTD

Why Do People Wish?

Make a wish. . . . Gaze at the first star of the evening and make a wish. Blow out all the candles on your birthday cake with one puff, and make a wish. Grab the end of the wishbone with a partner at the other end, pull, break, and if you get the larger piece, make a wish. There's also the moon, of course. And don't forget the four-leaf clover. And horseshoes.

But don't stop there. You can enrich your wishing life in more than five hundred twenty-five ways. Did you know about wishing on a rusty nail, a stubbed toe, or a "white rabbit night"? What about a dog, owl, butterfly, dandelion, apple, beard, snore, butter, or the mail truck?

Where do all these, and more, "wish-ons" come from? Why, from where else than from people—or "folk"? Several centuries ago, people may not have been exposed to theories of psychology or studies of the human

4

mind, but they had the same basic instincts as today's folk. If proof is needed, look to the remarks Aesop (620–560 B.C.; see page 188) and Seneca (8 B.C.–A.D. 65; see pages 180, 188) made about wishing. Wishing customs have endured for centuries, from the so-called unsophisticated past to today's enlightened entry into the twenty-first century.

Some rituals are ancient, some merely old, and many are modern. Old wishing customs can sometimes be found in books on folklore; modern ones are frequently communicated through the Internet. Most often, they are simply passed on by word of mouth. This is folk tradition at its most basic level. Word of mouth is more than a relic of the past; it is the primary means of communication among humankind.

Some rituals have been passed down with acknowledged places of origin. We know that certain practices come from England, or Europe, or Asia, or specific parts of the United States. Others have been so readily absorbed by other societies and subsequent generations that everyone identifies them with their own birthplace. Attempting to trace origins of most of these rites is virtually impossible. Even when a locale can be identified, it may not—strictly speaking—be the place of *origin*. Nor does it mean the particular custom exists only in that locale.

Not all ancient customs continue into future generations. But making wishes on wish-ons continues to thrive even in a society that has worldwide communication on tap. There has to be a reason for such longevity.

Perhaps the reason is its harmlessness; wishing on something doesn't hurt anyone. In fact it helps people by giving them a way to express their hopes and dreams. Just picture someone—an ancient peasant in a field or a modern executive in a corner office—hatching a wish-on, creating another item or circumstance to call up for the curious comfort that active wishing bestows.

Still, what is it about wishing that grips the human psyche? Psychologists speculate that the impulse to participate in wishing rituals is inherent—a natural longing for mystery—and a deep-seated desire for security or insurance. Even the most sensible and nonsuperstitious people admit to occasions when they have spontaneously made a wish—it is, in a sense, both an invocation and a simple declaration.

Many people consider the words *dreams, hopes,* and *wishes* to be word-cousins. The intent of something yearned-for within each term makes them akin to each other. There is, however, one basic difference. To dream and to hope are basically passive. To make a wish is active—to invoke a wishing custom requires a further step.

As a deliberate action, wishing is comparable to what modern psychologists term *affirmations,* or conscious statements—whether written or spoken—of the power to accomplish one's goals. The theory is that by concentrating on a goal, you subtly influence yourself to realize it. Goal-oriented affirmations are analogous to prayer—for those who believe—and to the *power of positive thinking,* a phrase coined in the early twentieth century. Some contemporary studies indicate prayer really does seem to affect recovery. The medical profession has long known that patients who believe they will get well have a greater recovery rate than those who do not. Comparatively, those who believe their wishes will be fulfilled are putting a positive spin on them. Creating affirmations, praying, and positive thinking are methods of self-fulfillment that help guide you toward accomplishing your goals.

What is a wish but a goal?

If you channel your wishes realistically, as you would your affirmations, prayers, or positive thinking, your wishes just might come true. Of course, if your wishes are directed toward wishing for a star to fall into your lap or having a long-lost relative appear with ten million dollars just for you, you're probably setting yourself up for disappointment. Direct your wishes at things within the realm of reason, and you just might create the affirmative aura you need to attract that job offer or lose that weight or whatever. If you make your wish often enough, you may find yourself actually doing what you need to do to make it happen. This is wish-fulfillment at its best.

The act of focusing through a wish-on, like a spider, maple seed, or rainbow, is simple reinforcement. You need not put stock in the magic of the object; but invoking the wishing custom reaffirms the desire. Few people would disagree that the best way to have a dream, hope, or wish come true is to frame it realistically, and then work toward getting it. Wishing on crickets, quilts, and yawns along the way are simply harmless reminders—positive visualizations that help us keep our goals in sight.

A review of the range of rituals reveals curious anomolies. Why does the number of species of animals to wish on far outnumber the kinds of birds? And why is it that people wish on zebras and magpies but not on monkeys or parrots?

It's clear why the letters Q, X, and Z have few entries; fewer words start with these letters. But why so few E's? How is it that C is the most frequent initial-letter of wish-ons? The second most frequent is S, with B, H, and W clustering next.

The serious anthropologist or folklorist, who studies social groups for an understanding of their desires, attitudes, and cultural values, is intrigued by the variety of wish-ons people have adopted. Added to that are the deviations in how they are supposed to be invoked. It's not unusual to find similar, but varying, customs even in a single region. Some wishing is straightforward—see the thing, make a wish on it. Many are accompanied by specific chants and/or actions, like walking backward. How, or why, did these chants and actions become attached to certain wishing customs, and why is the wish considered ineffective if the decreed accompaniment is not carried out in full?

Contradictions are numerous even on specific wish-ons: one custom requires the wish to be spoken out loud while another says it must be silent; one ritual demands a single statement while the next requires the wish to be stated three times. What it amounts to is that, with many of the customs, the wisher has a lot of latitude. You can pick and choose the things you prefer to wish on, and you have your choice about the accompanying ritual. Or you can invoke the method that suits you at the time. Wishing is, after all, a personal matter.

In quotations, proverbs, and verses, the wisher can find personal reinforcement. Alongside the encyclopedic A-to-Z listing of wishing customs herein, you'll find comments about wishing by writers and thinkers from William Shakespeare to George Bernard Shaw to Eleanor Roosevelt and many more. Proverbs have been framed by such historical figures as Benjamin Franklin, Francis Bacon, and others. In addition, there are verses, some humorous and some serious, by poets from Alexander Pope to Sarah Orne Jewett to John Dryden. Some take the realistic view, some compare wishing to prayer, and some speak to the importance of having dreams. In these, and in the rituals, taboos, and even language that has evolved from wishing, humankind has made its imprint. It's amazing to see how many and what kinds of things people wish on—cracked mugs, crossing state lines, zwieback. . . . And the list will continue to grow as long as humans are, well, human.

Lest we get too bogged down in psychological interpretations of wishing, we shouldn't lose sight of the simple fact that wishing rituals are fun. There's a certain beguilement in wishing, and certainly a charm. Finding ways to invoke wishes is good sport. For some wish-ons, you have to come across them, like a haywagon, empty barrel, or ladder. Others have to happen accidentally, like wishing on an eyelash or spilled salt. Other wish-ons are available to you any time, like amulets or the little indentation under your nose called the *philtrum*. For that matter, you can emulate the great

Scottish poet Robert Burns, who invented his own folklore, declaring he was as much folk as anyone else. There's no law against creating your own wishing traditions; after all, you too are folk. There are more than five hundred and twenty-five wishing customs listed herein; that number surely does not include the entirety of wishing lore. Other customs exist in special locales; many may live in secret, guarded places in peoples' hearts.

Though individuals may believe or disbelieve in the ritualization of wishing, participation is global. There's enough leeway in the semantics to serve as a catchall for what ultimately amounts to wishing; you can call your thoughts many things—dreams, hopes, goals, objectives, desires, aspirations, affirmations, prayers, or wishes. If you're human, you have them. How actively you avow them separates the wishers from the non-wishers.

Most people who go through the motions of wishing on wish-ons do so with a mixture of skepticism, playfulness, and hope. We may not believe in the spell itself, but there remains within us the primal impulse of the mystic.

May you find herein some rituals to make your wishing fun. May you make good wishes—and may all your wishes come true. So, go ahead . . . *make a wish*.

Acorn

When you see your first dropped acorn of the season, pick it up and make a wish on it. Keep it for good luck.

If an acorn falls while you are standing under an oak tree, pick it up, turn around three times, and make a wish. Put it on a windowsill for three days to make the magic stronger.

An old tradition calls for putting an acorn in the window so that Thor, God of thunder and lightning, will spare the house.

(SCANDINAVIA)

Albatross

If an albatross circles a ship, wish for good weather.
Long ago, an albatross circling a ship was thought
to be an omen of wind and bad weather; thus the wish
probably came about as a countermeasure.

Amulet

An amulet is a lucky charm or wish-on, usually worn or carried on the person, but sometimes considered effective just to own. Since the earliest times, people have selected certain items to serve as amulets, including bones, teeth, coffin nails, petrified wood, whalebones, shells, rocks, stones, crystal, numerous precious and semiprecious gemstones, weathered clothespins, crab or lobster claws, rabbits' feet, hair, coins, medallions, various articles of clothing, and jewelry including cufflinks, tie-tacks, pendants, brooches, rings, and so forth.

Usually, the object has been deemed a wish-on by virtue of being from a special place, being connected with a particular event, or being the gift of a particular person. These are purely personal amulets. Anyone can choose anything they like to serve as a personal amulet.

Some types of amulets have been adopted as more universal beliefs connected to wishing customs.

If you wish to have safe travel, you should wear a silver charm and rub it three times as the journey starts, while wishing for safe passage.

Any charm, jewelry, amulet, or other object that has given you good luck may be invested with special qualities. (The custom of wearing these is akin to wishing—the very act of empowering the object with the capability of bringing good luck is the same as wishing on the object for good luck.)

Frog charms are considered particularly fortuitous amulets for creativity or inspiration. Make a wish for either of these while stroking your frog charm; it is said that you must concentrate and believe.

This wish-on probably has its origins in ancient Egypt, Greece, Turkey, and Rome, where people looked on the frog as a symbol of creativity and inspiration.

If you have a turtle amulet (charm), hold it tightly in your hand as you make a wish. Some say the wish may be for anything; others say it must be for good health or a long life.

The ancient Chinese believed that the turtle was a sign of longevity.

(*See also* Clothes, Lucky; Coin; Rabbit's Foot;

Ring; Stone, Wishing; and Wishbone)

Apple

Two or more people should each tie an apple on a string (horizontally around the apple, with stem up). Next, swing the apples (now the stem will be pointing sideways). The person whose apple stays on the string the longest may make a wish.

After you eat an apple, take two of the seeds, hold them in the palm of your hand, and make a wish. Stick an apple seed on each of your cheeks. Keep your face very stiff. If the seed on your left cheek falls off first, your wish will come true. If the one on your right cheek falls off first, the wish won't come true. Neither will it come true if you deliberately make movements with your left cheek to make that seed fall off first! You mustn't speak aloud or make any vocal sound from the time you wish until the time the

first seed falls. (This trick is fun to do among friends—but remember, laughing out loud will keep your wish from coming true.)

Hold an apple's stem in one hand while you twist and turn the apple with the other about a quarter-turn each time. With each quarter-turn, count off the alphabet, "A, B, C, D . . ." When the stem breaks off, you should make a wish to marry someone whose last name starts with that initial.

(NORTH CAROLINA)

If you can break an apple in half with your bare hands,
you may make a wish to marry your love, and it will come true.

(KENTUCKY)

If you slice an apple into equal halves without cutting or nicking a seed,
your wish for love will come true.

Peel an apple in one long peel, make a wish,
and throw the peel over your left shoulder. If it forms one of
your own initials, your wish will come true.

*Throwing a long apple peel over your shoulder is also a way
to find out the first letter of your future sweetheart's name.*

Apple, Crab

If you can eat a crab apple without frowning,
you should make a wish as you swallow the last bite.

*Eating a crab apple without frowning is also supposed
to help you get your choice of spouse.*

(KENTUCKY)

Automobile

If you see an automobile with only one of its headlights lit, say "Perdiddle" and make a wish as you touch your nose. If there are several people present, the first to say "Perdiddle" gets to make a wish while tweaking another person's nose.

(PENNSYLVANIA)

If you see a car with only one of its headlights lit, hit your left palm with your right fist and make a wish.

If you see a red automobile, quickly pinch yourself as you make a wish. You must be finished making your wish before the car is out of sight.

When traveling by automobile, if you go either over a bridge or through a tunnel, put one hand on the ceiling of the car, and have the driver blow the horn as you make your wish.

(*See also* Bridge)

18

B

Balloon

If you see a balloon flying in the air, make a wish on it.

(See also Written Wish)

Balloon, Hot-Air

If you see a hot-air balloon in the sky, make a wish. Even if you can't
see the people in the passenger-basket, wave to them so they
can take your wish through the air as they fly.

Barrel

If you find an empty barrel, hold both hands against it as you make a wish.

If you see a truckload of empty barrels, make a wish on it.

Bat

Should you see a bat, make a wish for long life and happiness.
*This is no doubt based on the old Chinese
belief that the bat signifies long life and happiness.*

If a bat lands on your head, make a wish,
or the bat will remain there until it hears thunder.

Beard

If you're walking with someone, and you see a man with a beard,
the first person to say "Padoodle" gets to make a wish.

(MICHIGAN)

Bed

If you are the first to sleep
in a bed, make a wish.

(See House, New)

Bee

If you find a bee onboard a ship, make a wish.

(ENGLAND)

Beetle

If you see a beetle fall on its back,
quickly make a wish.

Bible

Make a wish before opening a Bible.

Bird

If a red bird flies in front of you, make a wish.

When you see a red bird, quickly spit three times.
If the bird has not disappeared from sight by the third spit,
you can make a wish.

If you hear a bird singing in the rain, make a wish.

If two birds fly toward you in unison, quickly
make a wish. If you finish your wish before they change
direction or pass you, it will come true.

If three birds perch together on one wire, make a wish.
If you finish your wish before any of them fly away, it will come true.

If you see a flock of birds, cross your legs and make a wish.

(ENGLAND)

If a flock of birds you didn't know was there suddenly rises from a field and flies over your head, quickly make a wish so the birds can take it with them.

(*See also* **Bluebird; Cuckoo; Eagle; Heron, Great Blue; Magpie; Ostrich; Peacock; Robin;**

Rooster; Swallow; Turtledove; Whippoorwill; New Year's Dove)

Bird's Nest

If you find an empty bird's nest, you get a wish.
If it has part of an eggshell in it, you get two wishes.

Birthday

*A wish made on your birthday has an
extra chance of coming true.*

On your birthday, you can make a wish on yourself. Cross your legs or ankles, cross your arms, and cross two fingers on each hand. Silently say: "I am. On this day of my birth I wish." Then make a good wish.

Within the first month of a newborn's birth, make a wish for his or her happiness, health, and long life. Cross two of your fingers and lightly touch the baby on the forehead as you make the wish. Wishes made within the first twenty-four hours of the baby's birthday are the strongest.

(*See also* Cake, Birthday; Coin; Clover, Four-leaf; Moon)

Blimp (or Dirigible)

A blimp is an airship without wings that looks like a giant football in the sky. If you see one, make a wish. Blimps fly slowly, but if you watch until it is out of sight, your wish might come true.

Bluebird

When you see the first bluebird of spring, make a wish.

Book

If you *accidentally* drop a book, put your foot on it and make a wish. Pick it up with the opposite hand from the foot, or your wish won't come true.

If you *accidentally* drop a book, or even see one on the floor that you did not put there, kiss it before you pick it up and make a wish.

Bridge

When you cross a bridge, make a wish and say:
"Bones, bones, sticks and stones,
Criss, cross, hear me bones."
*This probably comes from the ancient practice
of burying bones in the foundation of a new bridge
for good luck and also to make magic that will
keep the bridge from falling.*

Make a wish while crossing a bridge;
it will be granted if you do not speak aloud
until you are across.

If you go over a bridge you've never crossed before, lift your feet off the floor of the vehicle you're riding in and make a wish. (The driver, for obvious reasons, is not supposed to make a wish.)

If you cross a bridge in an automobile, hold your breath until you reach the other side and make two wishes: one as you get on the bridge and one before you get off. (A very long bridge might present a problem.)

When you cross a bridge you've never crossed before,
make a wish in the middle of it.

If you walk over a bridge you've never walked over before,
jump three times after every twelfth step, and you can make a wish
just before stepping off the bridge at the other end.

Breaking stride to jump while on a bridge may have its origin in the military practice of having troops "break cadence" while crossing bridges; the steady marching rhythms hammer the bridge's supports, which can be destructive.

If you walk over a bridge you've never walked over before, stop halfway across, look first upriver (or up the valley or ditch), then look downriver (or down the valley or ditch), jump three times, make a wish, jump three times again, look downriver, and then look upriver.

Helpful Hints

Some people believe that to get your wish you should do and say the following: "Touch blue and your wish will come true."

Some people spit three times after making a wish so the devil won't keep it from coming true.

After making a wish, count silently to twelve before speaking.

In some areas, three people agree to make the same wish, believing this will surely make it come true.

Many wishing customs require their own particular rituals: crossing fingers, spitting, waiting a certain number of hours or days, wearing something for a certain period of time, waiting to see something such as a car with only one headlight or a bearded man.

Spit three times from a bridge into the water as you make a wish.

Count to thirty-three by threes as you go over a bridge and then make a wish, repeating it three times.

If you go under a bridge, make a wish.(Another custom is to cross your fingers as you go under a bridge so that it won't fall down on you.)

(**See also** Automobile)

Bridge, Covered

If you are lucky enough to come across a covered bridge, stand outside the bridge and walk through it until you are on the other side (outside the bridge). Make a wish. Turn around and walk back to where you started and repeat the wish. (It is taboo to make your wish while you are under the roof of the bridge.)

Bridge, Draw

If you are stopped from crossing a drawbridge because it is up, you are entitled to make a wish.

If you see a boat go under a drawbridge, make a wish.

Broom

If a broom *accidentally* falls over, step on it and make a wish before picking it up.

(**See also** Mop)

Buckeye

If a buckeye (also called a horse chestnut or,
in England, a conker) falls from a tree you are under,
pick it up and hold it as you make a wish.
Buckeyes are supposed to be particularly effective
if the wish is to relieve a headache or other pain.
Some people carry buckeyes for good luck.

(OHIO AND PENNSYLVANIA)

Butter

If you *accidentally* get butter on your fingers,
make a wish. It doesn't work if you purposely
get your finger in the butter.

As you're passing butter to someone,
if you can get some butter on that
person's finger, you get a wish.

(WISCONSIN)

Butterfly

If you see a white butterfly, make a wish.
If the butterfly flies out of sight,
it is taking your wish to be answered.

If a butterfly lands on you, make a wish.
It will come true if you make the wish before
the butterfly disappears from view.

Button

If you find a button, wish on it and
put it away for seven days.

C

Cake, Birthday

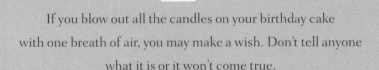

If you blow out all the candles on your birthday cake
with one breath of air, you may make a wish. Don't tell anyone
what it is or it won't come true.
(This is one of the most widely practiced wishing customs.)

The birthday person should make the first cut in the birthday cake,
making a silent wish while cutting.

(PENNSYLVANIA)

Cake, Wedding

When it's time to cut the wedding cake, the newlyweds should both put their hands on the knife as they make the first cut; each should make a silent wish while cutting.

As the bride and groom traditionally feed each other the first bites of cake, they should each make a wish for the other.

If you put a piece of wedding cake under your pillow, you may wish on it last thing at night and repeat the wish first thing in the morning, provided you have not spoken to anyone during that time.
Some say you will have good luck if you sleep with wedding cake under your pillow, and others say you will dream of a future love.

Camel

You can make a wish when you see a camel, but wishing on a camel can be tricky. Seeing how many humps it has is easy enough, but you have to know what kind of camel the number of humps signifies to make the wish effective. Here's a memory trick: the Dromedary camel has one hump; the Bactrian has two humps (a *D* has one hump; a *B* has two humps). In making your wish, you must address the camel correctly.

"Dromedary camel, here's my wish."

Say this once, for the one hump.

"Bactrian camel, here's my wish."

Say this twice, for the two humps.

Candle

If a candle goes out by itself before it has burned all the way down, quickly make a wish so the spirits can carry it to the wind.

This is also supposed to avert evil, or evil spirits.

Cat

If you see a cat eating grass, quickly make a wish, then turn away. If your wish is to come true, you mustn't see the same cat again that same day.

If you see a cat looking at a fire with its tail away from the fire, make a wish. Don't ever make a wish on a cat whose tail is toward the fire, or the opposite of your wish may happen.

If you see a cat washing its face, touch each of your cheeks
and then your chin; after that, make a wish.

If a black cat crosses your path, make a wish.

If a black cat crosses your path, say "Black cat, bring me luck."

If you meet a black cat, stroke it three times
from head to tail and then make a wish.
(This is more powerful than just seeing a black cat.)

If you see a white cat, make a wish after saying:
"White cat has fur,
Drinks milk from a dish,
White cat can purr,
And bring me my wish."

If the cat purrs as you are making your wish,
there is a good chance that your wish will come true.

If a gray cat crosses your path, this is a sign of very good luck;
you should strengthen the luck by making a wish for good luck.

If you see a three-colored cat, make a wish. Repeat it three times.

Should a calico cat be up in a tree, make a wish and say:
"Cat in a tree, This wish is for me."

The first time you meet any given cat, you should stroke it seven times,
repeating your wish with each stroke.

Cattle

If you see a cow or cattle lying down on Christmas Day, make a wish.

(EUROPE)

This no doubt has its origins in the belief that cattle kneel at midnight on Christmas Eve to honor the memory of Jesus Christ's birthday in a Bethlehem stable.

(*See also* Cow)

Chair

If a chair *accidentally* falls over, as you are uprighting it, hold it balanced in place on only one of its legs and make a wish.

After a pregnant woman has sat in a chair, if you want to have a baby, sit in the chair and wish to get pregnant. (A counterwarning to this: Don't sit in a chair recently vacated by a pregnant woman if you don't want to get pregnant.)

(PENNSYLVANIA)

Chestnut

If you have a chestnut, make a wish on it that involves something good happening to someone unfortunate.

Juggle three chestnuts, making sure each is lofted in the air at least three times. (More than three times is okay, but fewer invalidates them.) Give two of the chestnuts to others to wish on, and keep the third for yourself. All should be kept for three days before being wished on.

Chicken Heart

Make a wish as you chew and swallow a chicken heart.
Some say the heart should be swallowed whole.

Church (or Temple)

Make three new wishes on entering a new church or temple.

If you see a church you've never seen before,
go inside and make the same wish three times.

(IRELAND)

If you see a church you've never seen before,
place both of your hands flat on the front door.
Say your wish three times in your head.
Walk away without looking back.

Church Lights

If you see a candle or light in a church *accidentally* go out,
make a wish quickly, so it can travel with the light.

Clothes

When putting on a new, unwashed garment
for the first time, make a wish.

If you *accidentally* put a piece of clothing on backwards,
make a wish as you're changing it.

If you put a piece of clothing on inside out in the morning,
you should leave it that way until noon and then make a wish on it.

If you notice that part of your clothing (such as your collar)
is *accidentally* turned up, make a wish before turning it back down.

Clothes, Lucky

As with lucky charms, any clothes worn when you
had particularly good luck may be invested with special
qualities. The custom of wearing lucky clothes is akin to
wishing—the very act of empowering the garment with
the capability of bringing good luck is the same as wishing on the garment for good luck. The most frequent good
luck items are ties, underwear, socks, and shoes.

Cloud

If you see a cloud in the shape
of a camel, make a wish.
However, to dream of a cloud in the shape
of a camel is said to be bad luck; it means there will
be no rain and therefore a poor harvest.

Clover, Four-leaf

If you find a four-leaf clover, make a wish on it.
(This is the simplest ritual of many connected with the "lucky clover.")
A general tradition is that the four-leaf clover is considered
"lucky" and often carried as a talisman.

As you wish on a four-leaf clover, hold it over your head.

If you find a four-leaf clover, make a wish as you put it in your shoe.

After you have wished on a four-leaf clover, toss it away.

If you find a four-leaf clover, do not pick it,
but make a wish, and the chances of your wish coming true
will grow as the clover grows.

If you find a four-leaf clover,
say the following chant while touching each leaf in turn:
"One leaf for fame, One leaf for wealth,

One for a faithful lover, One for glorious health;
All in this four-leafed clover."
When you have finished saying the chant, twirl the clover between two fingers of your right hand and make a wish for one of the four things the clover
holds for you. (You can press the clover between the pages of a book.)

When you find your first four-leaf clover in spring,
eat it as you make a wish.

If you find a four-leaf clover on your birthday, pick it,
cradle it in your palms, and say:
"Birthday, four-leaf clover,
Now I turn you over. (Turn over the clover.)
Here's my wish." (Whisper the wish into your palm.)
A birthday clover is supposed to be especially powerful.

If you are unmarried, and find a four-leaf clover, put it in your shoe and
wish to find a sweetheart. If you've walked at least three hours with the
clover in your shoe, and all the leaves are still on the clover, your wish will
come true within three months.

If you find a four-leaf clover in any month but May,
pick it, make a wish, and put it in your left shoe.

If you find a four-leaf clover, pick it and then kiss it as you make your wish.
Put it in your shoe and remove it the day you want your wish to come true.

Put a four-leaf clover in your shoe as you make your wish; when the clover
gets lost, you will get your wish. (Clearly, it can only be "lost" by accident.)

When you find a four-leaf clover, pick it without breaking off any leaf, make
a wish on it, and carry it with you the next twenty-four hours. If any leaves
break off during these twenty-four hours, your wish will not come true.

Coal

If you find a piece of coal in the road, pick it up, spit on it,
throw it over your left shoulder, and wish. You will get your wish,
but it may be a long time before it is granted.
*Some people say that you mustn't look back at the coal
once you have thrown it over your shoulder.*

Coin

If you find a penny, make a wish on it. If you spend it, your wish won't come true. Some people keep them as lucky pennies, hoping that the longer they are held the stronger the chance will be that the wish will come true.

Instead of keeping a wishing-penny they have found, some folks put the penny where someone else can find it. It's a fun thing to do, and if the finder is also a penny-wisher who wishes on it, the chance of the original finder's wish coming true increases.

You don't have to find a penny to initiate a wishing-penny chain. You can make a wish on a penny and turn it into a wishing-penny by leaving it somewhere, hoping a penny-wisher will find it. (Even if the person's not a penny-wisher, lots of people consider a found penny a lucky penny.)

> **Proverbs:
> On Money and Work**
>
> Wishing won't do it,
> But saving will.
>
> Wishes never filled a bag.
>
> Wishers and Woulders are never
> good householders.
>
> Heaven helps those who
> help themselves.
>
> If you want to make a dream
> come true, wish for it;
> If you want to make a wish
> come true, work for it.
>
> Wish with a will
> and work with a will;
> So will your wish come true.

On your birthday, you should wear a silver coin in each shoe (even a partly silver coin will do, such as a dime); at the end of the day remove the coins and make an important wish. Coins kept and used annually gather more power the older they get.

(*See also* Amulet)

If you find a foreign coin, you should hold it between your index finger and thumb, and swing your arm in a large circle to signify the world. Then cup the coin between your palms as you make a wish.

(*See also* Fountain)

Color

Throughout the Caribbean Islands, a charming custom holds that certain colors can affect your destiny in specific areas of life. Sometimes colored beads or tiny colored-glass cylinder-beads are braided into a straw bracelet or necklace. There are always seven beads, though the wearer has the choice of wearing seven of one color for concentrated wishing or all seven colors for a general wish for good luck in all categories. Once a day, the beads may be stroked and a wish made that fits the colors.

Blue . . . . .Happiness
Green . . . . .Peace
Orange . . . . .Success
Red . . . . .Love
Purple . . . . .Fame
White (or clear) . . . . .Health
Yellow . . . . .Wealth

Comb

If you find a comb with the teeth pointing away from you, make a wish.
(If the teeth are pointing toward you, the comb is not a wish-on.)

If you *accidentally* drop a comb, point the teeth down and make a wish.

If you *accidentally* drop a comb, step on it as you make a wish.

Compass Directions

When you see a bathtub you've never seen before,
you can make a wish if it points north/south.

When entering a room you've never been in before,
you can make a wish if the floorboards run north/south.

(*See also* Moon)

Corn

Make a wish on a grain of corn
and bury the corn.

Corn on the Cob

If you have a cob of corn with either seven or fourteen rows, you can make
a wish as you take your first bite. (If you forget—too bad, wishes made on
anything but the first bite have no chance of coming true.)

Cow

If you see a cow slap its tail against a tree or fence, make a wish.

If you see an albino (all-white) cow, cross your fingers
and make a wish for something that has white in it or on it.

If you see an all-black cow, you should make a wish. If there is a herd of
them, there is a very good chance that your wish will come true.

(*See also* **Cattle; Quonset Hut**)

Cricket

A cricket in the house, particularly on the hearth, brings good luck; make
a wish on it. If the cricket chirps, your wish will come true.

(**ENGLAND**)

Cuckoo

When you hear a cuckoo for the first time in the season,
turn over your money and make a wish.

When you hear a cuckoo for the first time in a new place,
call out "cuckoo" three times and make a wish.

Dandelion

When you see the first dandelion of the season, make a wish.

When dandelions have dried to whiskery puffs, you should pick one, make a wish, and then blow on the puff. If you blow off all the whiskers in one puff, some will manage to fly away and fulfill your wish.

Blow on a dandelion puff and make a wish. Then say:
"Dandelion, puffs away,

Make my wish come true some day."
If all the "whiskers" are gone after the third puff,
your wish will come true.

(*See also* **Santa Claus**)

Dew

On the first day of May, go outside in the morning
and wet your face with dew as you make a wish.

If you find dew on a morning glory, wet your lips
with it and make a wish.

Dinnerware

The person at the table who gets a dish with a flaw or chip may make a
wish when taking the first bite of food. (Switching dishes so you will get
the "wish dish" invalidates your wish.)

If you are served a beverage in a cup or mug with a manufacturing flaw (a burr, off-center border or design, etc.), you should take your first three swallows from the reverse side of the cup, holding it with your left hand, and make a wish.

Another wishing custom regarding a flawed dish, mug, or cup is that the person receiving it must stroke the flaw three times while making his or her wish.

If there is one piece of cutlery from a set that has a manufacturing flaw (offset design, goudge, burr, etc.), the set should be placed in a large mug so the flawed portion is hidden; the person who draws the "lucky spoon" (or knife or fork) should tap it on the table three times while making a wish.

If you *accidentally* drop a knife, fork, or spoon,
make a wish before you pick it up.

·

Dishrag

Bury a dishrag as you make a wish on it. You mustn't tell anyone about it.

If you *accidentally* drop a dishrag, make a wish on it before picking it up.

If you drop a dishrag, step on it, make a wish, and then pick it up.

Dog

When you see a dog chase its own tail, quickly make a wish before the dog settles down. If it stops circling before you finish making your wish, your wish won't come true.

When you see a three-legged dog, spit three times,
then silently make the same wish three times.

If you hear a dog howl at night, make a wish.

(**See also** Horse, White; Ladder)

Dolphin (or Porpoise)

If you see a dolphin or porpoise jump out of the water three times, quickly make a wish. A wish made on a whole school of them

has an even greater chance of coming true.

For a couple to see two porpoises or two dolphins jump together is supposed to be a sign of compatibility. Each individual should make a silent wish that might affect the relationship in a positive way.

Fortunatus's Purse

Fortunatus was a hero of medieval Eastern legends who possessed an inexhaustible purse given to him by the Goddess of Fortune and a wishing cap he stole from the Sultan of Cairo. He traveled through many lands and led a luxurious existence. Upon his death, his sons inherited the purse and cap but, as a result of their foolishness and recklessness, fell upon hard times.

The theme of the tale is alternately interpreted as showing either the vanity of human prosperity or that people should place reason and wisdom before greed. Fortunatus appeared again in the 1509 German *Volksbuch (Folk Book)*, and in subsequent dramatizations of this tale.

The term *you have found Fortunatus's purse* means *you are in luck's way.* Another common expression, *needing Fortunatus's wishing cap,* means *needing some good luck.* The term *wishing cap* merely drops the name Fortunatus from the allusion.

Donkey

If you hear a donkey bray, make a wish. If it brays three times,

it will help your wish come true.

If you hear a donkey bray in the morning,
make a wish and recite this chant:
"Donkey, donkey, old and gray,
Open your mouth and gently bray.
Lift your ears and blow your horn,
To grant my wish this early morn'."
If the donkey brays again shortly after you say the chant,
your wish will have a better chance of coming true.

Door

When you stand before a door you've never gone through,
place your hands on it, and make a wish
before knocking or ringing the bell. If someone answers,
there is a chance that your wish will be granted.

(*See also* Church)

E

Eagle

If you see an eagle (try a zoo),
make a wish. If the eagle flies, there is a better chance
of your wish being granted.

If you see an eagle in the open air, this is very lucky
(but be sure it is not a hawk); make a wish, then chant:
"Eagle free, fly to make my wish come be."

Earring(s)

If you lose an earring, the one remaining has one wish in it for you.

(CALIFORNIA)

If someone gives you a pair of earrings,
make a wish the first time you put them on; the wish only counts
if you wear the earrings for at least three hours.

Ebony

Ebony is a hard wood, most prized when it is black.
It is frequently polished and made into jewelry.

Stroke a piece of ebony as you make a silent wish,
repeating it to yourself three times.

Egg

Make a wish with the first bite of an egg.

Egg, Good Friday

A Good Friday egg and the last egg of an aging hen have been considered lucky charms that protect the henhouse.

Make a wish on an egg laid on a Good Friday.

Proverbs: Wishes and Hunger

If wishes were horses,
Beggars would ride;
If turnips were watches,
I would wear one by my side.

NURSERY RHYME
(FIRST NOTED 1846)

One never fares worse than when one wishes for one's supper.

One must keep one's mouth open a long while before a wished-for roast pigeon flies into it.

He that lives upon hope will die fasting.

BENJAMIN FRANKLIN

Hope is a good breakfast, but it is a bad supper.

FRANCIS BACON

Elbow

If you *accidentally* bump your elbow, raise that arm into the air and make a wish.

If you *accidentally* bump your elbow on the spot known as the "funnybone," cross your arms so you can hold an elbow in each hand, and make a wish.

Elephant

When you go to a circus or zoo, be on the lookout for the first elephant you see, because that is the one you should look at as you make your wish. (An Indian elephant, which has small ears, is good, but an African elephant, which has large ears that droop below the tusks, is even better; the African elephant's ears are shaped like Africa).

A white elephant, which is rare, is said to carry strong magic
for making wishes come true, so be sure to make
a good wish if you see a white elephant.

Equator

If you are crossing the equator,
cross your fingers on each hand and wish.

Eyelash

If an eyelash accidentally falls out, you can make a wish on it. (It won't

57

work if you pull one out.) Put the eyelash on the back of your hand, close your eyes, and blow gently while you make a wish. Open your eyes. If the eyelash has blown off your hand, your wish will come true. (Your wish won't come true if you overdo the blowing.)

Put an accidentally fallen eyelash on the back of your left hand as you make your wish. Then, placing your left palm over the back of your right hand, hit your left palm with your right hand—three hard blows, with your eyes closed. If the eyelash is still there when you open your eyes, the wish won't come true. But, if one of the blows has knocked it off, the lash has gone to fulfill your wish.

If you or a friend accidentally loses an eyelash, press the eyelash between your thumb and your friend's thumb. Both of you make a wish. Separate your thumbs. The person whose thumb the eyelash sticks to will get his or her wish. If the eyelash falls to the ground without sticking to either thumb, neither of you will get your wish.

(JAMAICA)

Feather

If you find a black feather, stick it in the ground
so it stands up, and make a wish.

Fingernail

When you first notice a white speck
on one of your fingernails, you should say aloud:
"A gift, a ghost, a friend, a foe; A letter to come, a journey to go."
Make a wish, also aloud, to see or get one of those things.
Then repeat the verse.

If you discover specks on your fingernails,
make a wish, and say the following:
"Specks on the fingers—Fortune lingers;
Specks on the thumbs—Fortune comes."

When you trim your fingernails, make a wish on the cuttings before throwing them away where no one else can get them.

Fish

If you press your little finger against the wall of an aquarium and a fish comes right up to it, nibbling, you can make a wish.

You should make a wish on the first fishing catch
of the day, and chant,
"Hook it, crook it, Bee bye bilookit."

Some people believe that the first fish caught on a particular day should be wished on for good fishing and tossed back to bring luck for the whole day.

Foot

If your foot falls asleep, spit on your finger

and make a cross on the foot that is asleep as you make a wish.

(*See also* Itching)

Fountain

Throw a coin into a fountain

while making your wish.

Throw a coin into a fountain and make a wish.

Count the number of rings it makes on the water's surface.

If it is an even number, your wish will come true. If there are

an odd number of rings, your wish will not come true.

An Ancient Belief

The ancients believed that a wish would come true if it was made while looking at or touching something connected with riches or good fortune. This was called *sympathetic magic* or *like brings like*.

This is no doubt the source of such customs as wishing on pennies, two-dollar bills, the "silver" moon, and amulets.

Throw a coin into a fountain and make a wish.

After making your wish, look for your reflection in the pool.

If you see it, there's a better chance that

your wish will be granted.

Throw a penny into a fountain (it must be a penny, not some other coin) and wait until the water has stopped rippling and you can see your reflection before you make your wish.

With your back to a fountain, throw three coins over your head and into the water. With each splash you hear, repeat the same wish. If you hear all three splashes, the wish power in the fountain is strong for you.

(EUROPE)

Forgotten Objects

If you have forgotten something and must go back for it, you are entitled to a wish. (It won't work if you leave the object behind on purpose.) You should take time to sit down with the object, close your eyes, and count to ten before making your wish.

Frog
(or Toad)

If you find a frog when the moon is full,
make an "X" on the frog's head with a wet finger.
Look at the moon and make three wishes.

(**WALES**)

If you hear a frog at the midnight hour,
immediately make a cross with your finger, first on the back
of one hand and then on the back of the other;
then make a wish.

(*See also* Amulet)

Fruit

When you eat any variety of fresh fruit
for the first time in the season, make a wish.

(*See also* Apple; Apple, Crab; Kumquat; New Year's Eve;

Plum Pudding; and Strawberry)

Gargoyle

When you spot a building with a gargoyle on it,

make a wish and say,

"Beautiful gargoyle,

Bless my wish."

If the building has a lot of gargoyles,

you must choose only one or you will cancel your wish.

Gingko Leaf

The gingko tree, with its fan-shaped leaves, was grown

in temple gardens in ancient China, where it was regarded
as a symbol of longevity. Because it is such a hardy tree,
it is chosen to line the sidewalks in many cities.

A gingko leaf can be wished on if you have kept it for three months. Make your wish and then be sure you don't lose the leaf for at least another three months. The green leaf of spring is good, but the gold leaf of fall is even better.

Giraffe

Should someone happen to mention a giraffe, you can make a silent wish. There is no magic in the wish if you ask someone to mention a giraffe.

Goat

If you see a goat, make a wish. If you see more than three goats at a time, make the wish three times—this will make the wish stronger.

Goose

A goose that honks directly at you invites you to wish.

Make your wish quickly and run away.

(Beware: A goose can be nasty and nip at your legs.)

A wish made on a goose on May 1, which is

Mother Goose Day, has a powerful chance of coming true.

Make your wish and then shout at the goose:

"Mother Goose, Mother Goose,

Go and set my good wish loose."

If the goose runs away (as they usually do),

your wish may come true.

Gopher

If you see a gopher, quickly make a wish. If the gopher continues on his way, it didn't notice your wish, but if it turns and goes in another direction, it has gone to make your wish come true.

(SOUTHEAST AND WESTERN AMERICA)

Grass

A circle of grass that is greener
than the rest is a "fairy ring." Stand in the center,
turn three times, and make a wish. If the fairy ring stays,
it can be wished on once every three days.
*Though myth supposes that the fairy ring
is caused by fairies having danced on the spot,
it is actually caused by the growth of
certain fungi below the surface that
produce increased nitrogen.*

(For another wishing custom about

"fairy rings" *see* **Toadstool.)**

Grasshopper

When you see a grasshopper, make a wish.
If it hops three times after you make your wish and
then stops to rest, your wish has a good chance
of being granted.

Hair

Wish on a snippet of your own freshly cut hair. If you can combine freshly cut hair from three different people, the wish will have the greatest chance of coming true.

Sweethearts should combine hair taken from each other's combs and bury it as they wish for their love to last forever.

Make a wish for good luck as you touch the head of someone with red hair. The younger the person, the better chance of the good luck coming through.

(*See also* **Horse**)

Hairpin

If you find a hairpin, hang it on a nail and make a wish.
Some say the nail should be rusty.

If you find a hairpin, hang it on a wire or nail and make a wish as you say:
"Hairpin; wind spin."
If the wind ever blows the hairpin off the wire or nail,
the wish you made on it will come true.

If you find a hairpin, hang it in a tree and wish for a letter
from someone in particular.

Halloween

On Halloween day walk out the door backwards and pick up some dust or grass. Wrap it in paper and put it under your pillow that night. If you make a wish before falling asleep, it will come true.

Eat a crust of dry bread before going to bed on Halloween.
Any wish that you make will be granted.

Hay, Bale of

When you see a bale of hay, make a wish and say
"Bale of hay, bale of hay,
Make a wish and fly away."
(TENNESEE, ALABAMA, LOUISIANA)

Haywagon

There are a number of variations on how to wish
on a haywagon. Some say it is actually bad luck to see
a haywagon and not spit and make a wish.

If you see a wagonload of hay, you should make a wish.
(NEW ENGLAND)

If you see a haywagon, count to thirteen, and then make a wish.

Make a wish if you see a haywagon,
but you mustn't look back to see the wagon again.

Make a wish if you see a haywagon, and say:
"Load of hay, load of hay,
Make a wish and turn away."
If you see the same haywagon again,
your wish won't come true.

(WISCONSIN)

A similar chant has only slightly different words:
"Hay, hay, load of hay,
Make a wish and turn away."
Here, too, you must not see the same haywagon again.

(CALIFORNIA)

If you see a wagonload of hay, make a wish.
It will come true only if you don't see
the back end of the wagon.

(ENGLAND)

Heather

Either fresh or dried heather can be used to make a wish for peace and tranquility. Though the more common purple heather is good, white heather is said to be even more powerful.

Heron, Great Blue

The great blue heron is good for wishing about creativity in the arts (writing, painting, composing, etc.). If you see one, make a silent wish about such creative endeavors. If the bird flies close enough that you can see the blue underside of the wings, you can make the wish stronger by saying,

"True blue, Make my wish come true."

(SOUTHERN UNITED STATES)

Horse, Black

If you see a black horse, shake your fist at the horse three times while making a wish. If the horse looks at you, there's a better chance of the wish coming true.

If you see three black horses, shake someone's hand. (Shake your own if you're alone.) Make a wish and look away. If you see the same horses again, your wish won't work.

Horse (General)

If you see a gray horse, spit first,

then make a wish.

If you see a piebald horse (one that is spotted and more than one color), spit over your right shoulder, close your eyes, and wish. If you see the horse's tail, your wish won't come true.

(ENGLAND)

A spotted horse is considered to be particularly magical; if you see one, close your eyes to make your wish, then look back at the spotted horse again and say "so be it."

(*See also* Ladder)

Horse, White

If you see a white horse, cross your fingers and make a wish.

Some say if you see one white horse you will have bad luck
if you don't cross your fingers or stamp your foot once
and then make a wish.

If you see a white horse in the street, make a wish,
but don't turn or look back until you're sure the horse is gone.

(ENGLAND)

If you see a white horse, make a wish, then look around for a girl or
woman with red hair. If you see one, your wish will come true.

If you see a person with red hair, look for a white horse.
If you see one you are probably a lucky person.

Upon seeing a white horse, make a wish, cross your fingers,
and keep them crossed until you see a black dog.

Upon seeing a white horse, wet your finger and touch the sole
of your shoe. Say a poet's name and make a wish.

(ENGLAND)

When you see a white horse, make a wish,
lick your thumb, and press it into the palm of your other hand.
Stamp the wet palm with your fist while saying:
"Crisscross, white horse."
If you stamp one hundred "crisscross,
white horse's" your wish should come true in a month's time.
(In some places the chant is:
"Crisscross, white hoss,
Money for the week's done.")

When you see a white horse, make a wish and say:
"White horse, white horse, ding, ding, ding.
Grant my wish for a very good thing."
(In some places the chant is:
"White horse, white horse, ding, ding, ding.
On my way I'll find something.")

Horseshoe

Early horseshoes were made to hold seven nails—
seven is considered a lucky number.
The earliest horseshoe beliefs started in Greece,
where the first horseshoes were made during
the fourth century.

If you find a horseshoe, rub it seven times while making a wish.

If you see a horseshoe, spit on it, make a wish, and throw it over your shoulder. If you pick it up with your right hand, throw it over your left shoulder; if you pick it up with your left hand, throw it over your right shoulder.

(ENGLAND)

If you see a horseshoe, throw it over your head,
quickly put your hands over your ears, and make a wish.
(Some traditions say that if you toss a "wished-on" horseshoe,
you should not hear it land or see where it falls.)

(ENGLAND)

Make a wish for good luck
when you hang a horseshoe on a wall.
Just having a horseshoe hung is supposed
to bring good luck. You have two choices
of how to hang it: Hang it with
the ends pointing up, so it captures and
holds good luck for you. Hang it with the ends
pointing down, so the magic in the horseshoe
pours out good luck for you.

(UNITED STATES)

House, New

As you go through the door
of a new house, make a wish.

The first time you go into a new house,
go into the kitchen to make a wish.

When you first visit a new house,
touch the bathtub as you make a wish.

As you leave a new house
for the first time, stand with your back
to the front door and make a wish.

The first night you sleep
in a new home, make a wish as you
designate the four corners of your bed:
"North, south, east, west,
Now I wish, then I'll rest."
Then make the same wish four times
as you look at each corner in turn.

I

Icicle

Gather three of the first icicles of the season. Hold them in your hand as you silently make your wish three times. Then put the icicles under a bush and leave them there. When they have melted, your wish may come true.

Ides, Wishing on a Day of

The "ides" of the ancient Roman calendar fell on the 15th days of March, May, July, and October and on the 13th days of the other months.

Within one hour after midnight of an ides, and before speaking to anyone, you should cross your arms on your chest, touch each shoulder with the opposite hand, and silently make a wish, repeating it in your mind three times; then lightly nod your head three times before taking your arms out of the crossed position.

The quotation "Beware the Ides of March" is from Shakespeare's <u>Julius Caesar</u>. This wishing custom may have derived as a counteraction to the danger implied by the Shakespearean reference.

(ENGLAND)

Iguana

Catch an iguana, hold it by its tail as you say your wish out loud, then set it back on the ground and watch it until it is out of sight.

(MEXICO)

Itching

If your ear itches, you should cover the itching ear
and make a wish that only good will be spoken about you.
*A common belief is that an itching ear means
someone is talking about you.*

"I Wish I"

I wish I hadn't lost my socks,
I wish I had a golden box.
I wish I weren't afraid to ski,
I wish I had a magic key.
I wish I hadn't spilled the ink,
I wish I had a robe of mink.
I wish I were famous and rich—a star,
And life were like books and movies are.

GLORIA T. DELAMAR

A fairy tale princess "Capricious,"
Was given one million wishes.
She wanted them dearly,
Bud didn't speak clearly,
So instead she got one million fishes.

JUDY TUCKER

If your eye itches,
don't rub it. Cover it
with one hand as you wish
for something or someone
you'd like to see.

If your lips itch, press them
together and make a wish.

If your nose itches,
make a small "X" on the tip
and make a wish.

If the palm of your hand itches, scratch it
and say the following chant as you wish for money:
"Money itch, money itch,
Money itch, money come true."

If your hand itches (some say the right hand
and some say the left), rub it on wood as you wish
for money and say the following words,
naming the hand that is itching:
"Left/Right itching,
Rub it on wood.
Wish for money,
'Tis sure to come good."

A very old belief is that if your hand itches—usually the palm is specified—you will be getting money.

If your foot itches, you should stamp it three times
and wish to go to a particular place.

This no doubt stems from the belief that an itching foot means that you will soon travel.

Jacks

You can wish on jacks (the game of jacks, not the jacks from a deck of cards). Put three jacks in a triangle at least a foot apart. Bounce the ball down (as opposed to tossing it up), gather the three jacks in one hand, and catch the ball before it bounces again. If you can do this three times in a row, you are entitled to a wish.

Jail

As you pass a jail, quickly cover your eyes and make a wish.
Don't look back at the jail.

Jar

Before you open a new jar (of anything), hit it with a knife handle
against a table, three times, as you make a wish. If the jar opens,
you will get your wish; if it doesn't, you won't get your wish.

If a jar drops to the floor and does not break,
you may make a wish as you pick it up.

Jeep

If you see a Jeep, make a wish and say:
"Jeep, Jeep, four wheels deep.
Here's a wish for you to keep."

When you see a convoy of military Jeeps,
you may make three separate wishes, after which
you must say aloud "Jeep, Jeep, Jeep."

Cross Your Fingers

If you make a wish with crossed fingers, it is said that this briefly traps "the power" where the fingers meet. This gives you a better chance for your wish to come true.

People also say "Keep your fingers crossed for me" when they hope something in particular will happen the right way for them—the crossed fingers are a sign of good luck.

Saint Andrew's Cross

To make a Saint Andrew's Cross, cross your middle finger over your index finger. This is the most common way of "crossing fingers."

Cross of Lorraine

To make the Cross of Lorraine, place two fingers of one hand across the index finger of the other, just below the fingernail.

Patriarchal Cross

To make a Patriarchal Cross, place the middle and index fingers of one hand across the index finger of the other, with the upper middle finger placed right on the fingernail of the index finger. This is the "wish for your wish to come true" cross to use when wishing something for another person.

Greek Cross

To make a Greek Cross, place the index finger of one hand on top of the first knuckle of the index finger of the other hand, keeping the fingers at right angles to each other. This is also called a St. George's Cross.

Ancient Two-Person Greek Cross

In early days, two people would make a cross by one placing an index finger on top of the first knuckle of the other person's index finger. The first person would make a wish while the second person wished for the wish of the first person to come true.

Joker (playing card)

If you are dealt a joker, quietly stroke it (no one must notice) and make a wish.

Jockey

If you see a jockey wearing his jockey outfit outside
of the racetrack, make a wish.

Make a wish on a jockey who is wearing a number that starts
with the same letter as a color in his outfit. For example,
wish on a jockey dressed in orange who is wearing the number one
or on a jockey dressed in teal who is wearing the number ten.

Jug

If you can get a sound from a jug when you first blow into its neck,
you may make a wish. (If you slip your lower lip over
the front edge of the jug's neck and blow down over that lip,
there's a good chance you'll get a nice resounding echo.)

Kangaroo

If you see a kangaroo hop, quickly make a wish.

If you see a kangaroo with a baby kangaroo in its pouch,
make a wish.

Key

If you come upon a key that you could once use
but no longer can, you may make one wish on it. If you keep the key,
there is a better chance of your wish coming true.

If you find a key that someone else has lost,
make a wish before picking it up. If you find the owner, there's a good
chance of your wish coming true.

Keystone

*The keystone of an arch
is the wedge-shaped piece at the crown
of the arch that locks the other pieces in place.*

Touch the keystone of an arch and make a wish.
(It might help to have another person with you
to boost you up if the arch is high.)

Kilt

Should you spot a man wearing a kilt
in some country other than Scotland, make a wish.
If you can manage to touch the kilt, your chances of the wish
coming true are enhanced.

Kimono

If you see either a man or a woman wearing a kimono in public, in some area other than the Orient, make a wish. If you can touch the kimono, there's a better chance of your wish coming true.

King

If you see a king in person,
hook your thumbs together and make a wish.

If you see a real king on television or in a newspaper,
you should immediately make a good wish
for some other male person.

(*See also* Queen)

Kite

If you see a kite caught in a tree,
make a wish.

A kite entangled on telephone lines
entitles you to a wish. If there is at least one bird
on the line as well, there's a better chance
of the wish being granted.

Knee

If you *accidentally* bump your knee,
hold a hand on each knee as you make a wish.

If you *accidentally* bump your knee,
make a wish as you say, "Bee's knee; Knee be."

Kumquat

As you eat the first kumquat of a meal,
put the entire kumquat in your mouth (peel and all)
and make a wish as you chew it. You mustn't
bite it off in pieces, but it's all right to swallow it in
more than one swallow.

Ladder

In early religions, the triangle
was a symbol of life.
A ladder leaning against a wall or
tree forms a triangle. This may be why
ladders have come to be wish-ons.

If you see a ladder, cross your fingers and make a wish.

If you want your wish to come true, keep them

crossed until you see a dog.

(ENGLAND)

If you see a ladder and very soon afterward see four dogs,
you should cross your fingers and make a wish.

(ENGLAND)

If you see a ladder, cross your fingers and keep them crossed until
you have seen three dogs and three horses. Then make a wish.

(ENGLAND)

If you walk under a ladder, make a wish, then spit.

Ladybug (or Ladybird)

*(In England, ladybugs are called "ladybirds."
Say the chants according to your own preference.)*

Put a ladybug on the back of your hand. Say:
"Ladybug, ladybug,
Fly away home.
Your kitchen's on fire,
And your children will burn."

Make a wish, then gently blow on the ladybug once.
If she flies away, your wish will come true.

Another variation of the verse is:
"Ladybug, ladybug,
Fly away home.
Your house is on fire,
And your children will burn:
All but one, and her name is Ann;
She crept under the frying pan."

In some areas the verse goes:
"Ladybug, ladybug,
Fly away home.
Your house is on fire,
Your children are flown.
All but a little one
Under a stone.
Fly home, Ladybug,
'Ere it be gone."

If you find a ladybug with seven or more
spots on its back, shake your hand at it seven times
as you make a wish.

Lamb

If the first lamb of spring looks at you,
you are entitled to make a wish.

If a black lamb looks at you, you should make a wish.
(A wish on a black lamb is considered more powerful
than a wish on a white lamb.)

Leaf

A Japanese custom says,
"To catch a falling leaf means that you will have
twelve months of continued happiness."

If you can catch a leaf falling from a tree
before it touches the ground, you may make a wish.

Lightning

When lightning flashes across the sky, make a wish.

(PHILIPPINES)

When flash-lightning
(where the whole sky lights up) occurs before a storm
actually starts, make a wish on it.

When a lightning bolt makes a jagged streak in the sky,
quickly make a wish. If you can get your wish started
before the bolt completely disappears,
there is a good chance your wish will come true.

Hold your wish for the third bolt of lightning—
this is the most powerful one to wish on.

(*See also* Thunder)

Lightning Bug
(or Firefly, Glowworm)

Catch a lightning bug.

As you cup it in your hands,

whisper your wish to it.

Set it free. If it flies out of sight

instead of landing nearby,

it has gone to make your wish come true.

Put a lightning bug on the back of your

ring finger, as though it were the jewel of a ring.

Wish for some kind of jewel. If the bug glows,

you will get the jewel some day. If it flies away without

glowing first, you won't get such a jewel.

M

Magpie

If you see a magpie flying with its tail turned up,
quickly make a wish.

Mail Truck

If you are with someone else and you see
a parked mail truck, the first person who runs to it and touches
the post office emblem on the side gets a wish.
(In Scotland the emblem is a crown. In the United States it is an eagle.)

(SCOTLAND)

Manatee

This curious-looking aquatic mammal is supposed to bring luck to all who see it.

Should a manatee poke its head above the water
so you can see it, make a wish.

Mince Pie

Make a wish on the first bite of mince pie.

He Said/She Said

1. She: A realistic wish is not for the moon and stars, but for hot soup, good bread, and a peaceful night's sleep.

   He: A wish made from air is just air; wish from your belly.

2. He: Wishes come from the right brain of hopes and dreams; implementation comes from the left brain of logic and work.

   She: A wish is an idea waiting to be developed by both brain and heart.

3. She: It's not silly to wish; it's only silly never to dream, never to have goals that will enrich your life.

   He: Wishes give wings to our spirits.

   (HE: WILLIAM T. DELAMAR/SHE: GLORIA T. DELAMAR)

There is also an English tradition
that it is good luck to eat mince pie on each day
from Christmas through Twelfth Night.

Moon

If there's someone you haven't seen
for at least three days and you wish to see or
dream about that person, say the following
chant to the moon:
"I see the moon, and the moon sees me.
The moon sees someone, I want to see."
Then turn around three times
while saying the person's name three times.

If you suddenly glimpse the moon over your right shoulder,
make a wish and it will come true.

Some customs say the moon
should be glimpsed over your left shoulder.

Moon, Crescent

The following traditions about wishing on the moon apply only to a crescent moon. A "new moon" is waxing or growing, and its crescent ends point to the left. A waning crescent moon's ends point to the right.

When a crescent moon sits on the edge of the horizon, make a wish on it. You should then watch it disappear (or "set") beyond the horizon. If you leave before the moon disappears, your wish will not come true.

The silvery glow of a new moon (waxing crescent) makes people think of silver, so wishes for good fortune and business success should be spoken aloud as you shake silver coins in your hand or pocket. Then bow to the new moon three times—or nine times for triple good luck.

On the evening of your birthday, look at the moon and make a wish. A crescent that has tips pointing up means the moon may withhold your wish. Tips pointing down mean the moon is spilling open to send you your wish.

When you see a new moon, hold up a coin and wish for money for the
coming month. As the moon increases, so will your money.

(JAMAICA)

If you see a new moon—one you haven't seen yet that evening—over your
left shoulder and you have a silver coin in your pocket or purse, turn it over
as you make a wish. (Some say you need only turn your wallet or purse.)

When you see a new moon, make a wish and say:
"I see the moon and the moon sees me,
God bless the moon, and God bless me."
You must see the moon out in the open, not through a pane of glass.
Your wish should come true within a year.

(JERUSALEM)

If you want to be married, look at a new moon through
a piece of silk cloth, and make your wish by saying this chant:
"New moon, new moon, I hail thee,
New moon, new moon, please hear me.
New moon, new moon, if I'm to marry

Show me how many new moons there will be."
The number of moons you see through the silk is the number
of months it will be before you marry.

Moon, Full

At the stroke of midnight on the night of a full moon,
hold up your empty wallet or purse; turn north,
east, south, west, each time saying:
"Fill it up, Fill it up, Fill it up."

(PENNSYLVANIA)

*A full moon on your birthday means
you will have a full year of good luck.*

(*See also* Frog)

Moon, Full "Blue"

*The expression "once in a blue moon" means
that something doesn't happen often. A "blue moon" refers*

to a second full moon that occurs in one month.
(It happens about ten times in eighteen years.) The blue
moon is powerful to wish upon.

Make your wish while looking at the blue moon. Say:

"Blue moon, blue moon

True blue moon."

.

Mop

If a mop *accidentally* falls over, step on it and

make a wish before picking it up.

(*See also* Broom)

Mustard Seed

Take three mustard seeds, wet your finger,

and pick up the seeds with the wet finger,

keeping the seeds suspended upside down.

If they stay on your finger while you make your wish,

your wish will come true.

N

Nail, Rusty

If you see a rusty nail, touch it and make a wish. Leave the nail where you found it, but reverse the ends to make your wish come true.

Necklace

Someone else can make a wish if they turn the charm or pendant on your necklace to the back of your neck. (Or you can do that with someone else's neck charm.)

New Year's Day

If you hear a dove on New Year's Day
while you are walking uphill, you should wish
for good luck for the whole year.

On New Year's Day, make a wish for good luck
while eating black-eyed peas.

(SOUTHERN UNITED STATES)

On New Year's Day, make a wish for good luck
while eating sauerkraut and pork.

(GERMANY)

All year long, if any kind of fowl (chicken, duck, quail, turkey, etc.) is
served, its wishbone is tossed into the dining room chandelier, where it
will stay until the end of the year. (Some people just save them in a bowl.)
On New Year's Day, all the wishbones (also called *merrythoughts*) are col-
lected. Everyone at the table crosses their own arms across their chests
and holds onto a wishbone with the person to either side of them at the

dining table. At a signal from the host or hostess, everyone breaks the two wishbones they're holding, trying to get the larger pieces. You can make one or two wishes, depending on how well you do.

(ENGLAND)

(*See also* Wishbone)

Woodland Wishers
"Wish on the Little Folk"

Come the brownies from the wood.
Cross your fingers, knock on wood.
Elves in green come close behind,
Get a wish set in your mind.
Fairy wings now lightly swish,
Quickly, quickly, make your wish.

GLORIA T. DELAMAR

New Year's Eve

Swallow herring at the stroke of midnight on New Year's Eve while making a wish.

(SCANDINAVIA)

Swallow a grape at the stroke of midnight on New Year's Eve while making a wish.

Eat a grape for each chime of the clock at midnight on New Year's Eve, while making the same silent wish twelve times.

(PORTUGAL AND SPAIN)

Niagara Falls

Honeymooners toss coins into the Bridal Veil Falls at Niagara Falls and wish for long, happy marriages.

(CANADA AND UNITED STATES)

"Fairy Fair"

They'd knock on a tree and would timidly say

To the Spirit who might be within there that day:

"Fairy fair, Fairy fair, wish thou me well;

'Gainst evil witcheries weave me a spell!"

. . . And e'en to this day is the practice made good

When to ward off disaster, we knock upon wood.

NORA ARCHIBALD SMITH

Night (and Love)

If you want to see someone you love, you should utter that person's name twenty times, then, before going to sleep that night, wish twenty times to see that person again.

(UNITED STATES)

If you wish to dream of your sweetheart, the last words
you speak before going to sleep should be:
"All ye saints, be good to me;
In dreams let me my sweetheart see."

Night (and Sleep)

If you wish to be assured of a restful night's sleep,
you should make this wish as you turn out the light:
"From ghillies and ghosties
And long-legged beasties,
And things that go bump in the night—
Good Lord, deliver us."

Night, White Rabbit

Twelve times a year there is a "white rabbit night." It's the last night of a
month—or, you might call it the first midnight to morning period of a new
month. If you say "white rabbit" three times—sometime after midnight,
and before you speak to anyone—you may make a wish for good luck for
that month.

Another belief is that on the first day of any month,
before speaking to anyone, you must say
"white rabbits" for luck. Some say "hares
and rabbits," and some just say "rabbits."

(ENGLAND)

Nuts

If you find two nuts in one shell where there should be only a single nut
(almonds, brazil nuts, hazelnuts, etc.) share the twin with someone and
you can both make a wish. The first one who remembers to say "lucky nut"
the next morning will get his or her wish.

(RUSSIA)

If you find two nuts in one shell where there should be only a single nut
(almonds, brazil nuts, hazel nuts, etc.), eat one of them and throw the
other over your head as you make a wish. After you have made your wish,
you should not speak to anyone until you can answer "yes" to a question,
or your wish won't come true.

(ENGLAND)

Obelisk

If you see an obelisk (a monument such as
the Washington Monument that tapers up into a point),
you should make a wish on it. If you are close
enough to touch the obelisk as you make your wish,
there's a stronger chance of its coming true.

Ocean

An ocean may be wished on if you have not been
on its shoreline for three months. Say the following chant

after you make your wish:
"Ocean blue, ocean blue,
Here's my wish;
Make it come true."

OK Sign

The OK sign signals that "everything
is fine" or "that was good." It is made
by holding up one hand on which
the index finger and thumb form a circle.

Should someone flash an OK sign at you,
immediately make a wish. If you make the sign back at
the person, your wish will be stronger.

Olive

To wish on olives, you must eat three,
repeating your wish silently with each one.

Opossum

If an opossum (or possum) crosses in front of you,
make a wish, saying it three times. If the opossum
continues on its way, your wish probably won't come true,
but if the opossum changes direction, it is going
to make your wish come true.

(NORTH CAROLINA)

Origami

To wish for the good health of a person who is seriously ill,
make one thousand origami cranes to hang in his or her room.
Make the wish while making the cranes.

(JAPAN)

On July 1, origami papers with written wishes
should be hung from a branch (preferably of
a bamboo tree) so that two special stars
will read them and make the wishes come true.

The two special stars are, according to a Japanese legend, a young man and a princess who are in love but are allowed to see each other only once a year, on July 1, a special wishing day.

(JAPAN)

Ostrich

If you see an ostrich, make a wish while looking at it
and then turn away.

An ostrich feather is considered lucky. If you can touch one,
make a wish for good luck about something in particular.

(**See also** Peacock)

Otter

If you see an otter, make a wish.
If it swims toward you, it is acknowledging your wish,
and it may well come true.

Overpass

Make a wish while you are going over and
before you exit an overpass.

(**See also** Underpass)

Owl

Should you hear an owl hoot,
you may make a wish for wisdom.

Another custom says that your wish must be for wisdom
about a particular decision or issue.

P

Peacock

If you see a peacock, make a wish. If the peacock runs toward you,
there is a better chance of your wish coming true.

A peacock feather is considered lucky. If you can touch one,
make a wish for good luck about something in particular.

(*See also* Ostrich)

Peapod

Wish on a peapod that contains nine peas.

Wish on a peapod that contains nine peas and throw the pod
over either shoulder. Do not look back at it.

If you come across a peapod that contains nine peas,
make a wish and immediately eat the peas.

Philtrum

*The little indentation between your nose
and your lips is called the philtrum. It's something
you always have with you.*

To make a wish on your philtrum, put one of your little fingers into the
indentation; while gently stroking the area, silently make your wish three
times. The philtrum ought not to be invoked more than once a day.

Pie

Eat the point of a piece of pie last,
and make a wish on it.

Pin

If you find a pin with the point turned toward you,

make a wish before picking it up.

If you find a pin pointing toward you, pick it up and stick it into your clothes upside down. Make a wish and leave the pin in the garment for at least twenty-four hours.

If you find a pin, pin it at the left shoulder of your clothes and make a wish. The wish will come true when the pin comes out.

Aladdin's Lamp

"Aladdin's Lamp" is one of the stories in *The Arabian Nights Entertainments* or *The Thousand and One Nights,* a collection that dates to the ancient Orient; the earliest known texts are from 14th- or 15th-century Egypt.

Aladdin finds a lamp, and when he polishes it, a genie appears who grants him wishes. (In some versions, Aladdin also has a ring from which, when rubbed, a genie emerges, but the lamp alone appears in most contemporary versions.)

Aladdin wishes for a magnificent palace and great wealth. Eventually, he marries the Sultan of China's daughter. She inopportunely disposes of the lamp, and Aladdin's palace is transported to Africa. The lamp lies neglected and rusted until Aladdin regains it and returns to China with his wife and palace, whereupon he lives happily ever after.

The phrase *you must have Aladdin's Lamp* means *you possess much luck.*

If you are pricked by a pin that is in your clothing, take it out, make a wish, and put the pin back in.

Should you find a straight-pin outdoors, stick it in any tree and make a wish. Go back the next day. If the pin is still there, your wish will come true. Remove the pin and take it home with you.

Should you come across a straight pin outdoors, stick it into the nearest tree and make a wish. Check it seven days later (the same day of the following week). If the pin is still there, your wish will come true.

Place, New

When you first visit a new place, make a wish.

The first time you enter a building, pause in the doorway and make a wish.

Plum Pudding

Every member of the family who comes into the kitchen

(or any friend who happens by) while the plum pudding

is cooking stirs the pudding and makes a wish.

(ENGLAND)

When you take the first mouthful of plum pudding, make a silent wish.

Potato Chip

When you have a potato chip that has a bubble in it, put the whole chip in your mouth and chew exactly ten times. Make a wish as you swallow. If you swallow the whole chip at one time, your wish will come true.

(UNITED STATES)

Pretzel

The standard pretzel shape represents
a child's arms folded in prayer.

Hold a pretzel in one palm and strike it with the other hand.

If it breaks in three pieces, you get a wish.

(UNITED STATES)

Quarry

Stand near the edge of a dry quarry (it must have no water in it);
shout across it, "Quar-reeeeee," then make a wish.

If you come upon a quarry that is filled with water,
make a wish as you throw a stone into it.

Queen

If you see a queen in person, hook your thumbs together
and make a wish.

If you see a real queen on television
or in a newsreel, immediately make a good wish
on a female's behalf.

(*See also* **King**)

Queen Anne's Lace (or Wild Carrot)

Pick a blossom of Queen Anne's Lace
and hold it on top of your head as you make a wish.
Then toss the blossom over your right shoulder
and do not look back at it.

Quiche

Make a wish as you eat the last piece
of quiche on your plate.

Cut off the point of your piece of quiche, save it for last,
and make a wish while you eat it.

Quilt

If you buy or receive a quilt, immediately endow it with a wish
by stroking it as you say the wish in your head. It must be a wish
that will benefit all of humanity. Whenever you stroke the quilt
thereafter, your wish will be reinforced.

If you have a quilt that has belonged to a beloved baby,
make a wish on it and place it on top of your own blankets that night.

Quonset Hut

If you spot a Quonset hut,
blink three times and make a wish.

Should you see a Quonset hut within city limits,
make a wish ending with the wish that your wish will come true.

Make a wish if you see a Quonset hut and
a cow at the same time.

R

Rabbit

If a rabbit crosses your path, take three steps backward and turn away to make a wish. If you look back at the rabbit, your wish won't come true.

(See also Night, White Rabbit)

Rabbit's Foot

A rabbit's foot has long been prized as a good luck charm. The most powerful magic of all is said to be a left foot obtained from a rabbit captured in a cemetery.

If you have a rabbit's foot,
you should stroke it as you silently wish
and then say, "Good luck, good luck, good luck."

Swing a rabbit's foot over your head three times
and say the following before making your wish:
"Up in the air, swish, swish.
Rabbit or hare, grant my wish."

Rain

If it rains while the sun is shining,
you have the opportunity
to make a powerful wish.

(FLORIDA)

Rainbow

At the first sign of a rainbow, make a wish.

(ENGLAND)

When you see a rainbow, make a cross on the ground
with a stick or stone and then make a wish.

(SCANDINAVIA)

When you see a rainbow, wish for the same thing three times
as you look at the beginning, middle, and end of it.

(UNITED STATES)

You should make a wish for happiness when you see a rainbow.

(PHILIPPINES)

If you see a rainbow, you should make a wish for money.
*This probably has something to do with the legend that
there is a pot of gold at the end of every rainbow.*

(IRELAND, ENGLAND, UNITED STATES, AND ELSEWHERE)

When there is a rainbow-colored reflection—caused by crystal, a prism, an
oil spill, etc.—on the wall, the floor, or on any surface, put the back of your
hand on it so you can capture it in your palm. Close your eyes and make a
fist, trapping the rainbow inside; then toss it into the air as you make a wish.

When you see a rainbow reflection, capture it in the palm of your hand (as above), then quickly pretend to swallow it as you make your wish.

Ring

Endowing rings with the power to grant wishes has ancient foundations in the many "enchanted" or "magic" rings of folklore. The properties of these include restoring youth, curing diseases or other ill health, overpowering enemies, bestowing riches, and even rendering the wearer invisible.

A gold ring is said to possess the power to grant special privileges. The ring should be placed on the ring finger and stroked gently while you make your wish. A gold ring will lose its power if overused; it should be saved for very special wishes.

A gold wedding ring can be used to wish for a cut on a finger to heal. One custom is to rub the ring with the finger that has the cut; another custom says to rub the cut with the ring.

The gold wedding ring of a happy and virtuous woman can be used to wish for the healing of a sty on the eyelid; the ring should be gently rubbed on the sty while wishing.

On the first day of August, you should make a wish on your wedding ring. Twist the ring around two times as you make your wish. (The double turning, rather than the usual three, represents the two who made vows over the ring.)

Any ring with either a precious or semiprecious stone can be used to wish for imagination, quick wit, or success in some endeavor. While wearing the ring on one hand, the fingers of the other hand should hold the stone (as though pinching it). While thus holding the stone, make your wish. Conclude by tapping the stone three times.

This custom, with the requirement that the ring have a stone which must be tapped three times, carries analogies to "Reynard's wonderful ring" from Roman de Renart, *a 14th-century French tale. Reynard is a fox whose ring—which exists only in his mind—boasts a stone of three colors: red to make*

the night as clear as day, white to cure ill health,
and green to make him invisible.

If you want to have safe travel, touch a ring
while making a wish for safe passage.

Turn your ring three times as you make a wish not to get lost
while traveling. If the ring has a stone of some kind, the wish will be
stronger. The ring must be worn throughout the trip.
This is reminiscent of "Otnit's Ring,"
a German legend in which a stone has the power
to direct its owner to the right road.

If you put a ring on someone else's finger,
make a wish that is good for both of you.

Ring, Class

Turn your class ring when you first get it, and make a wish.

(UNITED STATES)

When you first get your class ring,
get as many people to turn it as the "class year"
(the last two numbers of your graduation year).
After the last person turns it, make a wish.

Robin

When you see the first robin of spring,
throw it three kisses and make a wish.
If you neglect to throw the kisses,
your wish will not come true.

Rooster

If you see a white rooster and he crows
as you look at him, make a wish.

Salt

Salt, now a staple, was once rare and precious;
it was even considered sacred by the Palestinians.
The ancients thought it had magic origins.

If salt is accidentally spilled at the table,
make a wish and throw a pinch of the salt over your left shoulder.

For three consecutive nights,
drop a pinch of salt on a fire (even a lighted candle will do),
making the same wish each night.

Plant a Seed

"Garden of Wishes"

Let your wishes adorn your daily life,
For wishes are fragrant flowers
That bloom in the garden of the mind.
The best wish begins
As a tiny seed of thought,
Expands to become a possiblity,
And finally explodes
In a reality of fulfillment.

GLORIA T. DELAMAR

"The Magic of Wishing"

Elusive as a fairy's shadow,
One small wish, uttered,
Stiffens the backbone of a dream;
Grants, even in the wishing,
Hope . . . the hope to dare . . .
To dare . . . to dream.

ETHEL S. OLIVER

"A Wish Can Be"

A wish can be a snowflake or a seed.
It can water the dream to succeed.
Will it melt to nothing
Or will it grow to meet the need?

WILLIAM T. DELAMAR

Samara

Samaras—known by many other names, including winged-seeds, winged seed heads, ash- or maple-keys, and colloquially as helicopters or angels' wings—are actually one-seeded winged fruits whose seeds never sprout, but remain closed.

If you find a samara
that has fallen from an ash, elm,
or maple tree, you can
make a wish on it.

After you make a wish
on a samara, put it on
the branch of a tree or on
a bush and leave it there.

131

A samara that actually falls on you as it wafts down is said to be a sign of good luck. Wish for something that would be good luck for you. Put the samara on the back of your hand and blow it off gently. It doesn't matter where it lands, but you must not pick it up again, if you want your good luck to come through.

A samara, because it looks like an angel's wing, is sometimes carried or kept as a good luck charm. The owner should stroke it three times when moved to make a wish. The longer it is kept, the more powerful it becomes.

An interesting custom connected with the samara is to gather some in the palm of your hand and make a wish either for the good of a deserving individual or for the good of the world. Keep this wish a secret, but give each of the samaras to others—they can keep it for good luck and to wish on, or they can give it to someone else, with the same suggestion that the lucky samara be kept or passed on. (Keeping the wished-on samara makes it grow more powerful for the individual. However, setting up a chain in which it is passed on sets up a force of communality that can affect the outcomes of all the wishes in a positive way).

(*See also* **Santa Claus**)

Santa Claus

The following out-of-season wishing customs
come from different areas of the same city; interestingly,
each uses seeds, but from different plants.

Blow on a dandelion puff (made up of dandelion seeds)
and tell Santa Claus what you want for Christmas.

(PITTSBURGH, PENNSYLVANIA)

Hold a winged-seed from a maple tree on the palm of your hand and blow it
away as you wish for what you want Santa Claus to bring you at Christmas.

(PITTSBURGH, PENNSYLVANIA)

Season, First Day of

The equinoxes and solstices are "season cross-over" times:
the spring/vernal equinox (about March 21); the summer
solstice (about June 21); the autumnal equinox (about
September 22); and the winter solstice (about December 22).

On the day that a new season begins, make a wish after the official "cross-over" time, while crossing your fingers. The closer to the exact time, the better the chance of your wish coming true.

Separate Paths

If you're walking with a friend and you each take a different path around a bush, tree, pole, rock, puddle, box, or anything else, hook little fingers with each other and make a wish. Finger wrestle. The one who makes the other let go will get his or her wish.

Shoelace

If your shoelace *accidentally* comes untied,
make a wish while retying it.

If your shoelace *accidentally* comes untied,
make an "X" on the ground and place your foot
(in the shoe with the untied shoestring)
on it while making a wish.

If you *accidentally* find that there is a knot in your shoelace, raise the shoe over your head three times (which you probably can't do if you're wearing the shoe) and make a wish. (Unfortunately, wishing that the knot will unknot itself doesn't usually come true.)

Make a wish if you tie someone else's shoelace.

Shoes

If you *accidentally* put your foot in the wrong shoe
(right foot in left shoe or left foot in right shoe), make a wish
as you put your shoes on the right way.

If you wish to dream of your sweetheart: Before you go to bed, place your shoes in a "T," with one shoe sideways at the tip of the other. With your hands on the shoes, say, "'T' wish; Be wish."

(A cross formed in the shape of a "T" is called both a Tau Cross and a Saint Anthony's Cross.)

Put salt and pepper on an old shoe and burn the shoe as you make a wish.

Before going out in new shoes, spit on them and make a wish.

Sky

If there are pink or red streaks in a blue sky, close your eyes
and make a wish.

Snake Track

If you see a snake track, spit on it, make a wish,
and rub out the track with your shoe.

(SOUTHEASTERN UNITED STATES)

Sneeze

If you sneeze only once, make a wish. Another sneeze
within three minutes will cancel the wish.

If you feel like you are going to sneeze, make a wish;
if you manage not to sneeze, your wish will come true.

Taboos

Some people believe that a wish should never be spoken aloud. This is the most prevalent taboo.

In some places it is taboo to speak at all after making a wish until you have silently counted to ten.

Some say "don't tell
your wish before breakfast."

(NORTH CAROLINA)

Some wishing customs specifically place a taboo on saying the wish aloud or telling it to anyone, but there are others in which the wish is meant to be said aloud. For example, when chants are connected with particular wishes they are most often said aloud.

A number of specific wishing customs have particular taboos associated with them, such as "don't look back," or "you must not see the thing again."

Many wishing customs are possible only if a circumstance has come about *accidentally*. It is absolutely taboo to deliberately create the situation, such as lose an eyelash, stub a toe, drop a book, or move around to the "other" side of a comb or pin, in order to have the chance to wish on it.

If you sneeze before getting up on a Sunday morning, make a wish.

If anyone sneezes at a table where thirteen people are seated, make a wish, then throw a pinch of pepper over your left shoulder to have a better chance of your wish coming true.

Snore

If you wake up hearing your own snore, make a wish.

(DENMARK)

Snowflake

Make a wish on the first snowflakes of a snowfall. Watch one particular snowflake drift down as you make your wish.

Spider

If you come across a spider, pick it up and throw it over your shoulder
as you make a wish. Be careful not to kill the spider or your wish
will most certainly not come true.

(ENGLAND)

If a spider spins its web
down in front of you, make a wish.

If you see a spider climbing a thread,
make a wish.

If you see a white spider,
make a wish before it disappears.

If you kill a black widow spider, you can make a powerful wish
if you say the following chant after you wish:
"Black widow spider, With red hourglass.
Black widow spider, I'll make my wish fast."

Squirrel

If a squirrel crosses your path, make a wish while you can still see it. If it runs up a tree there's a better chance your wish will come true.

Star

When the stars are out, choose the first star your eye catches sight
of (selecting is taboo!) and say the following verse:
"Star light, star bright,
First star I've seen tonight.
I wish I may, I wish I might
Have the wish I wish tonight."
Make your wish. A wish made on the "first star" should never
be told to anyone, or it won't come true.
(UNITED STATES AND MANY OTHER PLACES)

A lesser-known version is to select a star, say "Last star I'll see tonight," wish, and then close your eyes and turn away, making sure you don't see any more stars that night.

A variation of the above "first star" chant is that after making your wish, you must turn around three times, touch a tree, find another star, and then look back at the "first star" you wished on so that your wish will be answered.

(CONNECTICUT AND NEW YORK)

When you see the first star at night, make a wish and say:
"I see specks, specks see me,
I'll see somebody tomorrow
I don't expect to see."

Look fixedly at the brightest star, wink three times, wish to dream that night of the person you will marry, and go right to bed.

(UNITED STATES)

Count nine stars for nine nights in a row (if it's cloudy, you may have to start over), each night reciting out loud as you count:
"One, two, three, four, five,
Six, seven, eight, nine;
Wish be mine."

Then silently make your wish. Some say that on the last night
you should add, "And so should it be."

Star, Shooting

If you spot a shooting (falling) star,
quickly make a wish. If you finish the wish
before the star disappears, it will increase
your chances of the wish coming true.

If you see a shooting star, quickly call out
"Money, money, money." If you finish before it disappears,
you may make a wish for money.

State Line

If you cross a state line or country's border, while traveling by land vehicle
(bicycle, bus, car, train, etc.), make a wish three times out loud. (This is
one of the few times a custom dictates wishing out loud.)

(EASTERN UNITED STATES)

Statue

A statue's nose is lucky for you if you honor the person that it represents.
Stroke the nose three times as you wish for good luck.

(ILLINOIS)

Sticks

Get a small stick and spit on it.
Throw it over your left shoulder as you make your wish.

(ENGLAND)

Stone, Wishing

The wishing stone appears often in folklore; it must be used for good, not evil, or it will have no power.

A stone with a hole in it is a "wishing stone." After making your wish, place the stone near your bed or over a doorway. The stone retains its powers and can be wished on again and again.

The wishing stone with a hole in it probably derives
from the "hag-stone," a naturally perforated
piece of flint used as a charm against evil or hung
around the neck for good luck.

(EUROPE)

Any stone from a place that is a "spirit-home" to you
(close to your heart) can be endowed as a
"wishing stone." Rub the stone gently as you make
your wish. The more often it is used for good,
the more powerful it becomes.

This probably has its origins in Aetites or Eagle-stones,
also called gagites. These stones, found in eagles' nests,
were said to have magical properties.

(ENGLAND)

If you find a round stone, spit on it and
throw it over your left shoulder
as you make a wish.

(ENGLAND)

As you skip a stone across a body of water, make a wish. Count the number of times it skips. If it skips an even number of times, your wish will come true; if it skips an odd number, the wish will not come true.

Strawberry

When you eat the first strawberry of the season,
make a wish on it.
*The first strawberry is said to be magical,
as it has very likely been grown
specially for you by elves.*

(ENGLAND)

String

If you find a piece of string outdoors, wrap it around your finger and make a wish. Wear the string for at least three hours. If the string is red, green, or blue, there is a better chance of your wish coming true.

Sun

Make a wish for money on the sun when it is at its highest

(between noon and 2 P.M.).

Sunset

Gently pinch yourself
and make a wish just as the sun sets.

(STAR ISLAND, NEW HAMPSHIRE)

Swallow

It is a sign of good luck if
swallows build a nest on your property.
To ensure it, cross your fingers and
make a wish for good luck.

Taste, First

Every time you taste something for the first time,
you should make a wish.

(FRANCE)

Thimble

Wrap a thimble in a piece of cloth
(some say it should be silk)
and carry it around with you for three days,
making a wish each time you enter or leave any home.

Thunder

Make a wish on the first roll of thunder.

If you wait for the third roll of thunder and make a wish as it thunders,
there's a better chance of your wish coming true.

(See also Lightning)

Time

If you *accidentally* catch sight of a watch or clock whose two hands have come
together, quickly make a wish. (Clock-watching renders the magic void.)

If a digital clock or watch shows all the same numerals (2:22, 5:55, etc., or
even 22:22 for military time), quickly make a wish before the numerals
change. (Some say that if you look back at the watch or clock before the
numerals have changed, your wish won't come true.)

When a clock chimes an hour that is any factor of three (three, six, nine,
twelve), make a wish and finish it before the clock finishes chiming.

When your alarm clock goes off, make a wish
before you or someone else turns it off. (You may wish it hadn't
gone off, but it's too late for that wish to come true!)

When a grandfather clock chimes midnight, make a wish.

Toadstool (or Mushroom)

If you see a double mushroom or toadstool, stamp on it three times
and rub it into the ground with your shoe as you make your wish.

If you see a ring of mushrooms or toadstools (this is called a "fairy ring"),
stand in the center with your eyes shut and say out loud:
"Fairy ring, fairy ring, fairy ring,
Make my wish come true."
Then make your wish silently before opening your eyes.
If a friend is with you, the friend should stand outside the circle while you
are wishing and your eyes are still shut and say:

"Wishes come true
In a fairy ring."
This will make the wish more powerful. You and your friend can take turns
helping to complete the chants for each other.

(For another wishing custom about "fairy rings" *see* Grass.)

Toe

If you stub your big right toe, kiss your right thumb
and make a wish.

If you stub a toe (any toe), kiss the back of the hand that matches
the stubbed toe (right or left) and make a wish.

Tooth

If your tooth comes out, put it under your pillow and wish for money.
*(Sometimes the Tooth Fairy comes while
you are sleeping and exchanges the tooth for a coin
or two—but that's another custom.)*

149

If you have a tooth pulled, throw it over a house as you make a wish. (Should you want to throw and yet save the tooth, look for a small house and throw it to a partner on the opposite side who can watch where it lands, or throw it over a doghouse or dollhouse.)

Train

If you're passing under a trestle just as a train goes overhead, make a wish.

(UNITED STATES)

If you see a train going in reverse, make a wish.

(ENGLAND)

If you see a smoke ring coming from a train engine, you can wish once.
If you see two smoke rings, you can wish twice.

(ENGLAND)

Transportation

The first time you ride on a new means
of transportation, make a wish and say:
"Go with the wind,
Go with my wish."
(This includes a new automobile, new skates,
new bicycle, inline skates, etc.)

Tree, Wishing

The tradition of the "wishing-tree"
exists in many real-life locales, as well as
in fiction. Usually, a tree becomes
known as magical because something
significant happens near it, from historical
events to deaths. There is also a tradition
of sweethearts pledging their love beneath
certain trees, thus making them
their personal wishing-trees.

If you come upon a local wishing-tree, put both your hands on it and look up in the branches as you make your wish.

(BRITISH ISLES, EUROPE, CANADA, UNITED STATES)

If you find a wishing-tree, walk around it backwards three times while silently repeating the same wish three times.

You can turn a mature, full-grown elm into a wishing-tree: walk around it backwards three times before making your wish.

(ENGLAND)

If you and a partner can reach around the trunk of a full-grown pine tree and touch hands, you can each make a wish while looking up into the branches. The thicker the trunk, the more powerful the chance of the wish coming true.

(NORTH CAROLINA)

As you plant a new tree, make a wish that is not selfish or personal. The more significant the wish, the better the chance that the wish will come true. (If the tree dies, so does any chance of the wish coming true.)

A lone tree of one variety surrounded by a stand of some other variety is said to be charmed; touch it lightly with your fingers and close your eyes as you silently make your wish, then silently chant:

"Tree of wishes, bring your power to bear on my wish."

Truck

Stamp your foot and make a wish when you see a red truck.

If you see a blue truck, pinch someone (gently) as you make a wish.

Turtle

If you see a turtle, wet your finger and make a cross on the turtle's shell.

Make a wish and say the following words:

"Turtle shell,

Wish me well."

(Make sure it's not a snapping turtle,

or your finger will certainly not feel well.)

(*See also* Amulet)

Turtledove

When you hear the first turtledove of the season,
walk three times around the tree where the bird is perched,
repeating your wish each time.

Two-Dollar Bill

If you get a two-dollar bill, fold it three times and hold it
clasped between the palms of your two hands. While twisting your
palms three times (thus stroking the bill), make a wish.
Put away the two-dollar bill, still folded in three; don't spend it
for at least three weeks if you want your wish to come true.

(CALIFORNIA)

U

Ukelele

If someone lets you pluck three strokes on his or her ukelele,
you should silently repeat the same wish with each pluck.

(HAWAII)

Umbrella

If you see someone carrying an umbrella
on a sunny day, make a wish.

Make a wish if you see someone carrying a completely purple umbrella.

If you see a child carrying a child-size umbrella, make a wish.

If you find an umbrella, make a wish on it. If you find the owner, the wish will surely come true.

Umpire

Should you see an umpire scratch his nose, immediately make a wish. If he scratches again in a short time, there is a good chance your wish will come true.

If an umpire touches his head during a game, quickly make a wish; if he scratches his head, there is a better chance of your wish being granted.

Underpass

When you pass under an underpass on the road, make a wish before you are completely through. (An underpass is usually short, as it goes under a roadway. A tunnel is longer, as it goes through earth or rock or under water.)

(See also Overpass; Automobile)

Underwear

If you accidentally put your underwear on inside out, make a wish before you correct it. If you don't turn it right side out, there is no point in making a wish, because there is no chance it will come true.

If you discover that part of an undergarment is showing (bottom of slip, waistband of underwear, collar of undershirt, straps, etc.), make a wish and adjust the garment. If you do not correct the problem, your wish has no chance of coming true.

(*See also* **Clothes, Lucky**)

V-sign

("V" stands for "victory." It is made by holding up the index and middle fingers of one hand in the shape of a V.) Should someone flash a V-sign at you, immediately make a wish. If you are able to make the sign back at the person, your wish will be stronger.

(See also OK-sign)

Vegetables, First

As you eat the first fresh vegetable of the season, make a wish.

(See also Corn, Corn on the Cob; New Year's Day; Olive; Peapod; Yam)

Volcano

If you are standing on a dormant volcano
and it is possible to look down into the crater,
make a wish, repeating it three times.

Volcanic Rock

To wish on volcanic rock, place both of your hands on a chunk,
mound, or mountain of it as you make a wish.

Should you find a chip or stone of volcanic rock,
cradle it in your hands and make a wish as you say:
"From rock to ashes,
From ashes to rock."

Waterspout

*This is a rotating, funnel-shaped or cylindrical
spout of water on the surface of an ocean
which forms when a cloud of spray is torn up
by swirling winds.*

If you see a waterspout over the ocean, make a wish on it and then turn
your back. Count to three slowly before you turn to look for it again. If it
has gone away, it has gone to take your wish to be granted. If it is still there,
it is thinking about it, and your wish may or may not be granted.

**(CARIBBEAN ISLANDS, HAWAIIAN ISLANDS,
PHILIPPINE ISLANDS, AND MANY COASTAL AREAS)**

Waterwheel

If you see a waterwheel (perhaps at an old mill),
you should make a wish on it. If the waterwheel is turning,
there is a better chance of your wish coming true
than if it is standing still.

Pessimists' Proverbs

With wishing comes grieving.

If a man could have half his wishes, he
would double his troubles.

BENJAMIN FRANKLIN

Weather Vane

If a church has a weather vane,
make a wish on it.

Alas! What a number of wishes
have come to nothing!

Wishing is a wishful pastime.

DOUGLAS CARPENTER

Should you spot a weather vane
on a stranger's home or barn,
you should make a wish and chant:
"Weather vane winds,
North, south, east, west;
Point to the way
My wish is best."

Well, Wishing

Drop a coin into a well as you make your wish. There's a better chance of it coming true if you can see your reflection in the water.

Drop a coin into a well and make a wish. Listen for the plop when the coin hits the water. The deeper the well, the better the chance of your wish coming true.

Fill a cup with water from a well. Take three swallows of water from the cup while making your wish. Throw the rest of the water over your left shoulder. (If anyone gets splashed, your wish won't come true.)

(ENGLAND)

To make a wish at a well, walk around it three times, drop a small pebble in each time around, and each time whisper your wish into the well. It will be heard by the wishing well's resident fairy.

(ENGLAND)

Drop a small branch into a well as you make a wish.
If it floats, your wish will come true.

Drop a small pin into a wishing well as you chant:
"Pin, spin;
Wishing well
Wish me well."

Whale

Should you see a whale spouting,
you may make a wish.

Whippoorwill

Upon hearing the first whippoorwill of spring,
immediately take three steps backwards, pick up whatever
lies beneath your left heel, and make a wish.

When you hear the first whippoorwill of spring,
hold money in your hand and wish for more.

Wine

If wine is *accidentally* spilled on the tablecloth,
make a wish before it dries.

When a bottle of wine is finished, blow into the neck of the bottle and make a wish; the deeper the bellow, the stronger the chance of your wish bring granted. (To blow into the neck of a bottle, don't blow straight down. Keeping both head and bottle upright, rest your lower lip on the rim of the bottle and blow down across the lower lip into the opening.)

Wishbone, Chicken or Turkey (or any other fowl)

In all customs having to do with wishbones,
it is taboo to put a finger on the head of the bone
to give yourself a better grip. The person

*thus applying unfair leverage invalidates any wish
he or she would make. In some areas, the wish
automatically transfers to the other person.*

Two people should each grasp one end of a chicken or turkey wishbone.
Each person pulls on the wishbone while making a wish. The one who
gets the larger piece of bone (the one with the head on it) will get his or
her wish. The wish must not be told to anyone.

(UNITED STATES AND ELSEWHERE)

Another tradition in some places says that the person
who gets the shortest piece will be the first to marry.

Wait for the wishbone of any fowl (chicken, duck, quail,
turkey, etc.) to dry. Two people then grasp the bone and snap it.
The one getting the piece with the head on it must quickly say
"lucky break" and make a silent wish.

Two people each grasp one end of the wishbone
and make a silent wish as they pull and twist the bone util it breaks.

165

The person who gets the larger piece will get their wish;
the other person must tell what their own wish was.

(NEW JERSEY)

A wishbone should be dried in the sun
and kept for a long time.
Touch it any time you want to make a wish.

(ITALY)

(*See also* New Year's Day)

Words, Rhyming

If you accidently speak in rhyme, make a wish and then say:
"Make a rhyme, make a rhyme,
Make a wish before bedtime."

Words Spoken at the Same Time

There are several customs that say that
if two people say the same word at the same time,

they may each make a wish.
There are several ways it can be done.

Hook little fingers with each other and say:
"Smokes goes in, Smoke goes out.
Smoke goes up the chimney spout."

Hook little fingers with each other and say:
First Person: "What goes up the chimney?"
Second Person: "Smoke."
Both together: "May your wish and
my wish never be broken."
(Some say "broke.")

An alternative tradition very much
like the one above is for both people to say together:
"I say chimney, you say smoke,
Then our wish will not be broke."

After saying the same word at the same time as someone else, you should quickly lock little fingers of the right hand as you each make a wish. This forms a hooked cross that will hold the wish. Then each should speak the other's name.

An alternative custom is for one person to call out a word that the other must answer with a term that is closely associated with it, such as "cup" and "saucer;" "table" and "chair;" or "cow" and "milk."

Hook little fingers with each other and shake hands
up and down while saying:
"Hinky, pinky,
Red, white, blue.
Hinky, pinky,
Wish come true.
Hinky, pinky,
_____. (name a color)"

If you both name the same color, you can each make a wish.

(HOLLAND)

Face each other. Each of you should extend a hand
toward the other while you say and do the following:
"One, (hold out one finger)
Two, (hold out two fingers)
Three, (hold out three fingers)
Open, (hold out open palm)
Shut, (hold out a closed fist)
_____. (say and do either "open" or "shut")"
If you both say and do the same thing on the last line,
you can each make a wish.

If you and another person say
the same thing at the same time, you should
each make a wish; then, don't speak
until you see a mail truck.

An alternative to the above is to not speak until you see a mailbox. This
might happen sooner than seeing a truck, depending on where you live.

Worm, Woolly

If a woolly worm crosses your path, make a wish.

Written Wish

Write your wish on a small piece of paper and
put it in a balloon. Blow up the balloon,
rub it on your head to create friction, then stick
the rubbed side on a wall. (The static
should make it stick.) If it stays on the wall at least
three hours, your wish will come true.

Write out your wish and put it in a balloon.
Set it free to fly away. If it ascends high in the air, your wish
may come true; if it catches in something or comes back down,
your wish will not come true. A windy day works best.

Write out your wish on a slip of paper
and pin or prop the message on a holy or revered statue

in a place of worship. Your wish will come true for as long as it stays there.

(JAPAN, MEXICO, SPAIN, AND SOUTH AMERICA)

Write your wish on a narrow strip of paper and wind it around the twig or narrow branch of a tree. (Taping or tying it is taboo.) As long as the paper stays on the branch, there is a chance of the wish being granted.

(JAPAN)

Write out a wish and put it in an empty walnut shell. Wrap thread around it to hold the wish. Then bury the shell under a tree so the wish will grow.

(BOSTON, MASSACHUSETTS)

(*See also* Origami)

171

X (as a symbol for a kiss)

If you receive a letter with
an "X" in the signature, meant to indicate a kiss,
tap it three times with a finger
as you make a wish.

When you sign a note or letter with an "X"
to indicate a kiss, first touch your lips with one finger,
then touch that finger to the "X"
as you make a wish on behalf of the person
who will receive the letter.

X (the letter)

When you are reading, if you see a capital "X"
or a five-letter word with an "x" in it, you should interlock
your hands so that the knuckles meet and your fingers
form five "x"s. Bob your hands five times, make a wish,
and then bob your hands five more times.

Xylophone

Softly play each note on a xylophone up the scale
and then back down again (don't forget to hit the top note twice).
When you have finished, make a wish.

Y

Yam
(or Sweet Potato)

Eat three slices of raw yam,

making the same wish with each bite.

Yarn

If you find a scrap of yarn on the floor or ground,

pick it up and make a wish on it before you throw it away.

Yawn

If you can keep from yawning when someone
else yawns, you may make a silent wish.
If you yawn in the next fifteen minutes,
your wish will not come true.

Yodel

If you hear someone yodel, quickly
make a wish. The sounds
of the yodel will help carry the wish.
This is one custom where it is okay to get someone
to yodel just so you can wish.

(SWITZERLAND)

Yogurt

Make a wish as you eat yogurt if you are eating
it as the hour-mark passes.

175

Yo-Yo

If you are going to use a yo-yo you've never used before,
make a wish before you start playing with it.

Yule Log

When you light the yule log for the first time at yuletide,
make a wish for the coming year.

(SCANDINAVIAN COUNTRIES, GERMANY, AUSTRIA,

SWITZERLAND, AND OTHERS)

Some people do not burn their yule log
but place a candle on it instead, which they light
each night during the yuletide season. Each time the candle
is set aflame, a wish can be made.

Z

Zebra

If you see two zebras standing close to each other,
make three separate wishes. If they do not move away
from each other, all three wishes may come true.

Should you see two or more zebras
running together, make a wish and chant:
"White and black,

Black and white;

That's my wish;

Make it right."

The more zebras there are,

the better the chance of your wish coming true.

Zipper

If you *accidentally* break a zipper, make a wish.

If your zipper *accidentally* gets stuck, make a wish.

(You may want to wish that it will unstick.)

Zoo

When you go to the zoo, you should walk

through the entranceway backwards while making a wish;

when you leave the zoo, walk through the same entranceway

backwards while making the same wish. If you forget

the second part, you forfeit your wish.

Zwieback

Put a piece of zwieback on a table and
hit it with your fist. If it breaks into two pieces,
you may make a wish. Say the wish two times,
each time touching one of the broken pieces two times.
(The two pieces, two touches, and wishing twice
probably stem from the word *zwieback*,
which means twice-baked.)

Wishing Wisdom
What to Wish For

There is no beautifier of complexion, or form, or behavior,
like the wish to scatter joy and not pain around us.

RALPH WALDO EMERSON

I wish you all the joy that you can wish.

WILLIAM SHAKESPEARE

No one can have all he wants, but
a man can refrain from wanting what he has not and
cheerfully make the best of a bird in the hand.

SENECA

It was a high speech of Seneca (after the manner of the Stoics) that, 'the good things which belong to prosperity are to be wished, but the good things that belong to adversity are to be admired.'

FRANCIS BACON

Do not wish to be anything but what you are,
and try to be that perfectly.

St. Francis de Sales

Hitch your wagon to a star.

Ralph Waldo Emerson

When you consider revenge, the hurting retort, the dastardly deed—
it is wiser to wish it done and let it go, than to do.

Douglas Carpenter

No wise man ever wishes to be younger.

Jonathan Swift

Wish Not, Want Not

I respect the man who knows distinctly what he wishes.
The greater part of all the mischief in the world arises from the fact
that men do not sufficiently understand their own aims.

Johann Wolfgang von Goethe

Happy is the man who early learns the wide chasm that lies
between his wishes and his powers!

JOHANN WOLFGANG VON GOETHE

The apparently irreconcilable dissimilarity between our wishes
and our means, between our hearts and this world, remains a riddle.

JEAN PAUL RICHTER

As it asketh some knowledge to demand a question not impertinent,
so it requireth some sense to make a wish not absurd.

FRANCIS BACON

Men whose dearest wishes are fixed on objects
wholly out of their own power, become in all cases more or less
impatient and prone to anger.

SAMUEL TAYLOR COLERIDGE

Many of us spend half our time wishing for things we could have
if we didn't spend half our time wishing.

ALEXANDER WOOLLCOTT

Who has many wishes has generally but little will.
Who has energy of will has few diverging wishes. Whose
will is bent with energy on one, must renounce
the wishes for many things.

JOHANN KASPAR LAVATER

To a resolute mind, wishing to do is the first step toward doing—
but if we do not wish to do a thing it becomes impossible.

ROBERT SOUTH

Early successes are mostly rather according to wish than wisdom.

THOMAS LYNCH

We Are What We Wish

Our wishes are the true touchstone of our estate;
such as we wish to be we are. Worldly hearts affect earthly things;
spiritual, divine. We cannot better know what we are
than by what we would be.

JOSEPH HALL

What ardently we wish we soon believe.

EDWARD YOUNG

We easily believe that which we wish.

PIERRE CORNEILLE

In idle wishes fools supinely stay; be there a will,
and wisdom finds a way.

GEORGE CRABBE

Our blunders mostly come from letting our wishes
interpret our duties.

ALEXANDER MACLAREN

Like our shadows, our wishes lengthen
as our sun declines.

EDWARD YOUNG

Things don't change, but by and by our wishes change.

MARCEL PROUST

There is nothing more properly the language

of the heart than a wish.

ROBERT SOUTH

He had his nest of wishes piping

to him all the time.

GEORGE MEREDITH

Wishing and Spirituality

Every wish is like a prayer with God.

ELIZABETH BARRETT BROWNING

Not what we wish, but what we want,

oh, let thy grace supply.

JAMES MERRICK

Let not that happen which I wish,

but that which is right.

MENANDER

It is probable that God punishes the wrong wish as truly as he does the actual performance; for what is performance but a wish perfected with power; and what is a wish but a desire wanting opportunity of action.

ROBERT SOUTH

A prayer in its simplest definition is merely
a wish turned God-ward.

PHILLIPS BROOKS

God, if You wish for our love, Fling us a handful of stars!

LOUIS UNTERMEYER

Look bravely up into the sky,
And be content with knowing
That God wished for a buttercup
Just here, where you are growing.

SARAH ORNE JEWETT

But long as god-like wish, or hope divine,
Informs my spirit, ne'er can I believe

That this magnificence is wholly thine!
—From worlds not quickened by the sun
A portion of the gift is won.

WILLIAM WORDSWORTH

Flavia's a wit, has too much sense to pray;
To toast our wants and wishes is her way;
Nor asks of God, but of her stars, to give
The mighty blessing, 'while we live, to live.'

ALEXANDER POPE

He gained from Heav'n
('twas all he wished) a friend.

THOMAS GRAY

On Wishes Granted

Hope [a wish], like the gleaming taper's light,
Adorns and cheers our way.

OLIVER GOLDSMITH

If you have built castles in the air, your work need not be lost; that is where they should be. Now put the foundations under them.

HENRY DAVID THOREAU

The future belongs to those who believe in the beauty of their dreams.

ELEANOR ROOSEVELT

Don't regret the foolish wishes you have made;
consider them the learning ground for making wiser ones.

DOUGLAS CARPENTER

Do not ask for what you will wish you had not got.

SENECA

We would often be sorry if our wishes were gratified.

AESOP

There are two tragedies in life. One is not to get
your heart's desire. The other is to get it.

GEORGE BERNARD SHAW

Granting our wish one of Fate's saddest jokes is!

JAMES RUSSELL LOWELL

Our very wishes (when realized)
give us not our wish.

EDWARD YOUNG

Mankind, by the perverse depravity
of their nature, esteem that which they have most desired
as of no value the moment it is possessed,
and torment themselves with fruitless wishes
for that which is beyond their reach.

FRANCOIS DE SALIGNAC DE LA MOTHE FÉNELON

Now obey thy cherished secret wish.

WALT WHITMAN

If wishes would prevail with me,
my purpose should not fail with me.

WILLIAM SHAKESPEARE

Index

Note: Index entries do not duplicate entries shown alphabetically in the body of the text (except when they also appear as sub-entries under other headings).